Building a Lemonade Stand is Not Just For Kids Anymore

Building a Lemonade Stand is Not Just For Kids Anymore

Entrepreneurial traits and resources for developing a business

Dulce M. Ramirez-Damon
and
Concepcion L. Tuma

iUniverse, Inc.
New York Lincoln Shanghai

Building a Lemonade Stand is Not Just For Kids Anymore
Entrepreneurial traits and resources for developing a business

iUniverse, Inc.

For information address:
iUniverse, Inc.
2021 Pine Lake Road, Suite 100
Lincoln, NE 68512
www.iuniverse.com

ISBN: 0-595-33041-X (pbk)
ISBN: 0-595-66734-1 (cloth)

Printed in the United States of America

Contents

Acknowledgements

This would not be possible without the unconditional support of many people. The following is not a hierarchy since each person made their own unique contribution and none could stand above the others in that regard.

To my husband Charles, who after 15 years of love and support—10 years of married life together—provides me with strength and purpose in life. I love you baby!

To Charlie, my 6-year-old son, whose constant smiles, hugs and kisses gave me the energy to work late at night on this endeavor. Charlie, you are my inspiration. I love you!

To my parents, who instilled the importance of working hard to achieve my dreams. You filled my life with morals and values and taught me the value of integrity and education. Thanks Mom and Dad! You are always supportive, regardless of how crazy my ideas seem. I love you both!

To my sister Rosa and my brother Carlos who taught me that we all have our own award-winning recipe for life. I love you! Thanks!

To my friend Sonya: Thank you for your honesty and timely feedback. You always validate and support what I do.

To my high school teacher, Maria M. Fernandez, who saw my potential early on, applauded my innovative ideas, and dreamed this before I did. Mrs. Fernandez, thank you for believing in me.

To my colleagues Connie and Adam: you are a breath of fresh air—and look at where it brought us. I value our friendship and collegiality.

Last but certainly not least to God, with whom ALL things are possible!

—Dulce

This book has taken over my life for many months, and, without the support of various people, it would have not been possible.

To my husband Michael: You are my inspiration, my everything in life. Thank you for valuing all that I do and for holding my hand every step of the way. I hope I make you as proud as you've made me. I love you!

To my parents: Thank you for showering me with unconditional love and support. From you, I have learned never to compromise my values and to be morally just in all that I do. You laid the foundation and I built the dream. You are the force that drives my success. Thank you for always telling me to "go for it". I did! I love you!

To my sisters: You are all goddesses I look up to. I have been able to learn and grow from your examples of love, generosity and perseverance. I hope to be living up to all you expect of me. Thank you for being the greatest gift God has ever given someone. I love you!

To Dr. Gavilan: Thank you for encouraging me to out-do myself time and time again. You made me feel important and you helped me grow into the professional I am today. From the bottom of my heart, Thank you!

To my colleagues Dulce and Adam: I am truly blessed to have friends like you. Thank you for all the hard work and dedication that has helped bring this endeavor to fruition.

To God: Thank you for enlightening me with the ability to put my knowledge on paper. I truly believe that with YOU all things are possible!

—Concepcion

Preface

Tired of thinking for your boss, writing the plan, and doing the work, but reaping none of the financial benefits? Have your ideas been rejected and then resurfaced—as your supervisor's brilliant brain wave—months down the line? Fed up with working 50 or more hours per week for someone else? Want to start your own business but you are afraid to take the plunge?

Building a Lemonade Stand is Not Just For Kids Anymore is filled with practical advice on every aspect of starting a business, along with useful tools, a glossary of terms, web sites, checklists and self-assessments to guide you along the way. The book offers candid advice and valuable resources for enterprising individuals that Dulce M. Ramirez-Damon and Concepcion L. Tuma each searched for when they left the corporate world behind and started working in higher education with the ultimate goal of starting their own companies.

When they met, both realized their talents were going to waste, and were afraid of suffering skill atrophy. They chose to combine their more than 20 years of experience in the corporate setting, and formed Who's That Enterprises, Inc., a consulting firm offering training and development seminars for aspiring entrepreneurs in the areas of Leadership, Ethics, Emotional Intelligence, Organizational Culture, Diversity Training and Motivation. Damon and Tuma are Doctoral students and continue to work in the Career Center of the institution they attend.

Damon and Tuma vowed to record their entrepreneurial journey and create a how-to guide for other entrepreneurs. The guide provides information on how to launch your own business, starting with the question *Are you the one to run the show?* From writing a business plan to knowing the legal implications of operating a business and, finally, getting your product on the market and selling it.

This book presents entrepreneurship as a combination of skills and self-discipline. It challenges the reader and pushes the aspiring entrepreneur to stand up, walk to the nearest mirror and ask *Am I ready to be the boss?* It creates an awareness of the role of emotional intelligence and personality traits; the importance of self-assessment; and it emphasizes the need to nurture an idea from start to finish.

So here is your copy of *Building a Lemonade Stand is Not Just for Kids Anymore*. See how you too can turn lemons to lemonade!

Introduction

○ ○

"Free enterprise will work if you will."

—Ray Kroc, founder, McDonalds

In *The Great Boom, 1950-2000: How a Generation of Americans Created the World's Most Prosperous Society,* historian Robert Sobel tells the captivating story of the last 50 years, when American entrepreneurs, visionary leaders, and average citizens transformed our depression-haunted and war-ridden society into today's thrusting economy. A half-century in which Kemmons Wilson of Holiday Inns, Ray Kroc of McDonalds, and other entrepreneurs like them catered to the growing post-war population by providing vacation options and food places for both the resident and the visitor.

Those were the days of the entrepreneur, usually a man who, with the family, owned and operated a small grocery store or coffee shop. His customers were constant and he knew their name. His primary focus was to provide services or products that would interest his locals.

Today, things have changed. Entrepreneurs come from all walks of life. According to the Center for Women's Business Research, the number of privately held women-owned businesses in the U.S. grew by almost 11 percent between 1997 and 2002. The center also found that more than half of Asian-American and African-American women who owned small businesses said their firms have grown over the past three years, a commendable accomplishment in an economic downswing. Consequently, the entrepreneur of the future is more likely to be more ethnically and culturally diverse.

In addition, women and minority entrepreneurs have gained visibility and recognition. High-profile figures such as Oprah Winfrey, Wally Amos of Famous Amos Cookies, and Bob Vila, serve as examples for many thinking about starting their own companies. Because there are more minority role models in business, it is increasingly seen by minorities as a viable career option.

Moreover, as newspaper headlines were blaring about the innovation that went hand-in-hand with entrepreneurs and dotcom ventures, the public became increasingly aware of start-up businesses and the risk-taking, innovative mind-set that defines the entrepreneur.

Students' working while going to school is not news. Due to financial pressures, college students have always worked and many have created their own enterprise on campus. What's different today are the forces both on and off campus that are leading even more students to set up shop. One of those forces is downsizing. Many students see their parents and their parents' friends worrying about keeping their jobs. That makes the idea of starting a company more attractive even if it begins in their dorm room. Another effect of downsizing is a reduction in the number of corporate recruiters pitching jobs on campuses. The last three years has posed many challenges for on-campus recruiting programs. Employers are doing more with less and students feel they are going to have to invent their own careers.

While uncertainty may be one side of the new economy, the other side is an abundance of opportunities. Technology in particular is a valuable tool for campus entrepreneurship. Not only does technology allow small companies to compete effectively against large ones, but the new generation of students are every bit as comfortable with computers as their parents were with television sets.

Finally, many more colleges and universities than ever before have formal entrepreneurship programs. That means more faculty advisors for young entrepreneurs, more fellow students helping with market research, more ties to the world of venture capital and financing opportunities, and more role models as teachers who are both teaching and running their own companies.

In addition, these same institutions see the potential of donations from wealthy alumni. They sponsor competitions, create entrepreneurial research centers and academic tracks. They too are being entrepreneurial in creating programs that will gain nationwide recognition.

Are business schools the only ones responsible for producing entrepreneurs? What happens to the music major longing to start a record label? Who plays a role in nurturing the entrepreneurial spark of non-business students? Are entrepreneurs born or made?

The more you explore this arena, the more you will discover that becoming an entrepreneur is not easy. **It takes** hard work, dedication and focus. **It takes** an idea: one that has not been thought of before. **It takes** the knowledge that a group of people have a need you can satisfy. **It takes** financial stability—initially you may be paying out of pocket for start-up expenses. **It takes** drive—you will be the sole employee of your new business venture. **It takes** dedication. **It takes** the ability to deal with rejection and **it takes** someone who has the courage to bounce back after failure.

Before taking the plunge into entrepreneurship, you have to make sure you have what **it takes**. If you can answer Yes to what **it takes** then you are ready to embark on your journey to create your own job and *Think Beyond the Lemonade Stand*.

1

Are you the one to run the show?

o o o o o o o o o o o o o o o o o o o o o o o o o o o o o o o o o
*"There will come a time when big opportunities will be presented to
you, and you've got to be in a position to take advantage of them."*

—*Sam Walton, founder, Walmart, Inc.*

Entrepreneur comes from the French word *entreprendre*, and means *to undertake*.
An entrepreneur is a person who organizes and manages a business undertaking,
assuming risk for the sake of profit. An entrepreneur is someone who can:

a. Recognize an opportunity

b. Use time, skills and money to add value to that opportunity

c. Handle the uncertainty of running a business

Recognizing an opportunity

The thing that makes entrepreneurs successful is the ability to see the unseen.
The ability to having a vision of improving something that already exists or creating something new. Successful entrepreneurs are creative and innovative. They
are able to think about a problem or a product until an idea comes to them. They
are then able to find a reasonable solution and capitalize on that.

Using time, skills and money to add value to an opportunity

Opportunities present themselves to everyone every day but those who know how
to capitalize on them are the entrepreneurs. Time and effort need to be put
together to come up with a business plan and marketing campaign. You need to
be able to put your idea in writing, whether to present it to a bank for financing
or to present to potential business partners. Entrepreneurs need to have the skill,

time and money to start their business on their own. The venture becomes an individual goal; the entrepreneur is usually alone.

Handling uncertainty

The entrepreneur's competition is the entire world and technology continues to make it difficult for entrepreneurs because it makes it easier for others to compete. The game plan is set. You know what you want to do and how, but do you know what lies ahead? Running your own business brings all sorts of headaches: legal questions, tax problems, patents, copyrights, insurance and possibly even bankruptcies. Entrepreneurs need to foresee the unforeseen and expect the unexpected.

Are entrepreneurs born or made?

Some may argue that entrepreneurs are born; others may argue that they are made. Many would agree that there is such a thing as an entrepreneurial mindset. This book will emphasize a combination of both innate and learned entrepreneurship. An entrepreneur needs to have a balanced combination of natural mindset and prolonged exposure to business ideas.

Are individuals born with specific characteristics that predispose them to entrepreneurial ventures? Is there a set of traits that can be linked to an entrepreneurial personality? What role does environmental context play? Does early exposure to entrepreneurialism create entrepreneurs? These questions are common topics of inquiry and debate among researchers in the field.

According to Cohen (July 1980), entrepreneurs commonly share certain personality characteristics. These include: restlessness, independence, a tendency to be a loner, and extreme self-confidence. Other researchers characterize them as innovative, action-oriented, high on need for personal control and highly autonomous (Schein, 1994).

A few of those skills seem to be things that are learned but others are innate, such as the ability or willingness to take risks. A person can either be a risk-taker or not.

Many educators would argue that entrepreneurs are made: that, while the entrepreneurial mindset is necessary, without some sort of training or exposure to the business world, the individual will just be someone craving a chance to change, and the business skills taught in school can make or break an entrepreneur's chance of success.

The mindset is most important because ideas, creativity and vision must come from the source: the entrepreneur. Entrepreneurs reach for the unreachable.

If the entrepreneur does not have the skills needed to run a business, this can be offset by hiring staff or consultants while becoming more knowledgeable whether by education or training. While we do not encourage hiring anyone until your business gets off the ground, we do encourage the idea of obtaining help for what you are weak on.

Successful entrepreneurs will be able to think and react in an environment that is fast-paced, rapidly changing and highly uncertain. Able to think of adding value to something already existing, or of creating something new. Able to make valuable suggestions and embrace change. Quality, too, is important to entrepreneurs because their compensation is directly geared to the success of their business venture.

The skills necessary to succeed are: organization and planning; marketing and product knowledge; management and financial knowledge; willingness to lead and work alone; and the willingness to take risks.

Organization and planning

What is the business venture being tackled? Will it be a sole proprietorship, a partnership, or a corporation? Will it be taking over a family-owned business, or building a home-based business? An entrepreneur needs to be able to answer these questions and more. The answers will determine the style of management and the capital requirements.

Organization and planning is the most important part of beginning a business. Deciding on the type of business to open and completing the required paperwork and forms is a huge undertaking. Taxation planning should not be neglected.

Marketing and Product Knowledge

In order to be successful, the business must have something to sell, must know the customers it wants to sell to, and how the product or service will be sold. First, begin by asking is the idea a good idea? If the answer is YES, then to whom will it be sold?

Marketing is not just about posting flyers, building websites, and advertising; it is about building a solid relationship with your customers. You must know several things:

- The size of the market for your product or service

- The types of competing products
- The business's strengths and weaknesses
- The likely customer reaction
- The improvements you might need to make.

A good way to start to analyze the market is by looking at the four P's of strategic marketing: Product, Place, Price and Promotions.

Product

The first thing to do is determine what is going to be sold. Does the product have value? Does the product already exist? Why would consumers purchase this product? Make sure the venture is a solid one.

Second, know the competition. What are they selling? How different or how similar is it to what you are selling? What are they doing well and what can they improve on? Why is their business successful or unsuccessful? What will make their customers want to buy from you? Research the competition in order to improve on their techniques, learn from their mistakes, and improve the competitive advantage.

Place

The product is now available. How is a physical location for the product or service found? Keep in mind it does not always have to be a physical office location. Look on the Internet and research the potential of creating a website to sell the product.

These are a few things that need to be considered when looking for a physical location for the product:

- Where does the business need to locate?
- Will there be a need for any renovations?
- Can the location grow with the business?
- Will the company be buying or leasing the space?
- What types of businesses are there in the area?
- What are the advantages and disadvantages of the area?

If designing a website for the business to sell and market its products and services is the best route, then most of the same questions are viable for making the Internet the location for the business:

- What will the URL name be?
- How many pages, and what features, are needed?
- Will the site be leased each year or for a longer term?
- Who will update the website? Is this something that needs outsourcing?
- What are similar businesses doing on their websites?
- What are the advantages and disadvantages of an Internet storefront?

There are many questions to ask and answer. The more these options are analyzed, the better equipped you will be for making the right decisions. No one said opening a business was going to be easy. However, the idea and the drive will enable the business to get off to a good start.

Price

Once the product and the place to sell are established, the next thing to think about is price. As economists would say, price depends on supply and demand. In English, it means the price should be something the target customer can afford. The more people know about the product, the more the price can be reasonably increased. Remember to calculate the amount of money it costs for the product and to take into account the time spent on research. How much are they selling the same or similar products for? It is very important not to under-price because it may lead the customer to think that the quality of the product is inferior.

Promotion

Once the business has the product, the location, and the price, it is on its way! Promotion is the final step. The type of promotion needs to be specific to the product and the targeted customers. Some examples of promotional ideas include telemarketing, and cross-promotions. Remember to market the product using the information found regarding the customers. What makes them buy? Where do they buy? What makes the customers different?

Have a solid strategy! Develop a marketing plan to get customers to buy the product. Research the strengths and weaknesses and use them to develop marketing objectives. Determine the short and long-term goals required to meet the marketing objectives. Develop marketing strategies and determine pricing. Once that is all done, get to work and make the business a successful one!

Management and Financial Knowledge

Do I have the management and financial knowledge needed to run a business? Contrary to popular belief, the entrepreneur does not need to be an expert manager or an expert accountant. What is needed is *business* expertise. As the owner you set the goals, determine how to reach those goals and make all necessary decisions. Although knowledge in management and financials is very useful, the business may be able hire someone to do those things. While the day-to-day money handling may be easy to learn, an accountant will be able to fill out necessary paperwork for social security and taxes.

Record keeping becomes the most important aspect of any business. Many businesses fail because of inadequate records or due to the owner's failure to use the information that was available. Without records, the advance of the business cannot be seen or forecast. Up-to-date records may forecast impending disaster, thus providing a warning where steps may be taken to avoid it. While this entails extra work, you will be more than repaid for the effort and expense.

If you are not prepared to keep adequate records or have someone else keep them, do not try to operate a small business.

Willingness to lead and take risks

Willingness to lead and take risks is the key to running and operating a business. With very few exceptions, every business begins as a small business. Some stay small while others grow as the years go by. Entrepreneurs are driven by success. They need to be persistent and confident that the venture will go well. Starting and managing a business is not easy, it is full of challenges and problems, and it is the ability to cope with disappointment and frustration that will determine success or failure.

2

It is all about the E.Q. not I.Q.

Discovering the Entrepreneurial Spark

What makes someone an entrepreneur is a complex question. What major characteristics do entrepreneurs demonstrate? What determines if someone is an entrepreneur or not? What is it that motivates people to start a business? These are all complex questions about *entrepreneurship* and they have been the subject of a great deal of study and research.

While starting a business may sound exciting, it is not something to take on lightly. Initially a self-analysis, and a little soul-searching, is imperative, to ascertain if that is the path to follow.

Entrepreneurship takes many forms. The business may develop a product or create a service. It could become an independent agent for an existing corporation. You may invest in a franchise or buy an existing business. You can even become an intrapreneur operating autonomously within a company.

Many people become entrepreneurs because they want to create something they own, to have a sense of personal accomplishment. Some view entrepreneurship as the key to becoming wealthy. Others want to separate from the corporate rat race and be their own boss.

However, operating a business is a tremendous responsibility. Employees depend on the boss to provide stable employment. Customers expect delivery on promises. Suppliers and lenders expect invoices to be paid. Investors want the business to turn an acceptable profit. Are you a person that can handle this kind of pressure? Are you willing to seize the opportunity and assume responsibility and not call it a day at 5 p.m.?

The Role of Emotional Intelligence

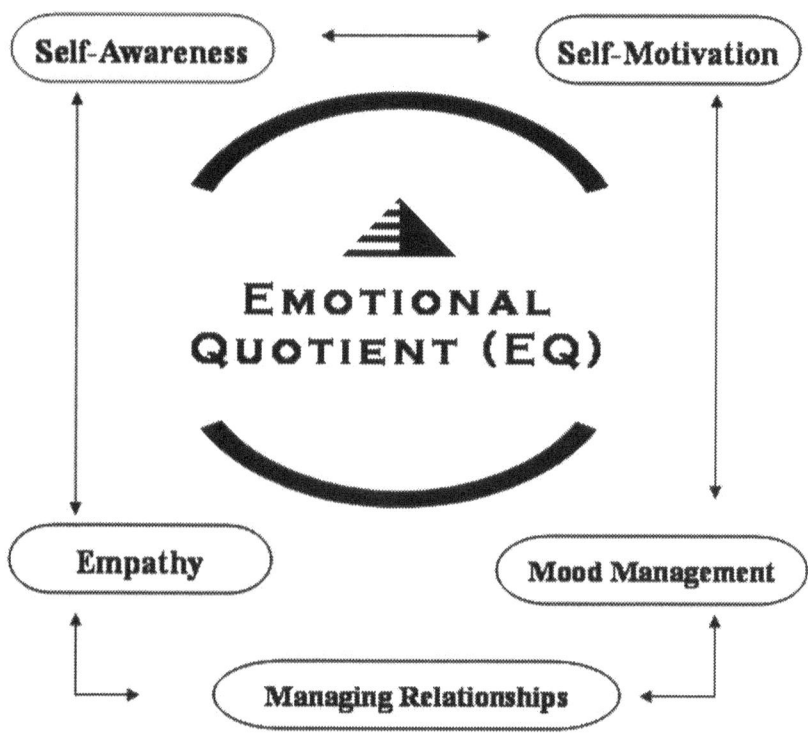

Emotional intelligence encompasses the following five categories: self-awareness, self-management, self-motivation, social awareness, and social skills.

Emotional intelligence emerged as a combination of different ideas in the 1980's with Howard Gardner's books *Frames of the Mind* and *Multiple Intelligences.* The concept of intelligence as a wide range of talents, not measurable by traditional spatial intelligence tests, was slowly becoming known through research. In 1990, Dr Peter Salovey of Yale and Dr John Mayer of the University of New Hampshire began publishing articles about something they called emotional intelligence. They tested how well people could identify emotions in faces, abstract designs and colors, and from these studies, they believed they discovered a sort of universal aptitude for emotions. They eventually published an article in which they outlined what emotional intelligence was, drawing together under one umbrella a series of what seemed unrelated skills.

However, the person most commonly associated with emotional intelligence is Daniel Goleman, author of the book *Emotional Intelligence,* published in 1995. By his definition, emotional intelligence is the capacity for recognizing our own feelings and those of others; for motivating ourselves; for managing emotions both in relationships and in ourselves. Emotional intelligence has now made its way from the classroom into the boardroom, tying into corporate business.

The concept of emotional intelligence can be summarized as a set of basic principles. According to Daniel Goleman, emotionally intelligent people have the ability to marshal their emotional impulses; they have the self-awareness to know what they are feeling, and are able to think about and express those things; they have empathy for the feelings of others and insight into how others think; they can delay gratification; they are optimistic and generally positive; they understand easily the dynamics of a given group, and, most important, where they fit inside that group.

Much of the difference between outstanding leaders is linked to emotional intelligence. It contributes to effective performance at work, outstanding leadership and deeply satisfying relationships in life. The characteristics of emotional intelligence are divided into personal competencies and social skills. Personal competencies are: self-awareness, self-management and self-motivation. Social competencies are: social awareness (empathy) and social skills (effective relationships). Emotionally intelligent entrepreneurs are able to manage both themselves and others. It is important to keep in mind that emotional intelligence is all about handling and managing emotions.

Self-Awareness: Recognizing feelings as they happen.

Understanding and recognizing our emotions is an important aspect of self-understanding and insight. Entrepreneurs who understand and embrace their feelings are better at what they do because they have a better sense of how they really feel about the personal and professional decisions that they make.

Self-Management: Handling feelings appropriately.

Self-management is imperative because of the need to handle uncertainty. Entrepreneurs face many trials and tribulations and they need to be able to manage their feelings so that they are mindful, when making important decisions, of whether feelings are in the way. Entrepreneurs who lack self-management may be overwhelmed with feelings of distress and aggravation; those who do not are able to bounce back no matter what happens.

Self-Motivation

Self-motivation is the essence of all entrepreneurs; it is what keeps them going. Self-motivation allows entrepreneurs to be highly productive and effective in their business ventures. It is about controlling emotions and delaying gratification in reaching goals.

Social Awareness

Recognizing emotions in others (empathy). Empathy is a very important people skill. Having social awareness allows the entrepreneur to understand and be more attuned to the subtle social and economic signals that indicate customer wants and needs. It allows the entrepreneur to better focus the business venture, not only to better themselves and their investment but to better cater to their customers, thus building long-lasting relationships which foster a greater and more loyal following for their business.

Social Skills

Building and keeping relationships goes hand in hand with social awareness. Excellent social skills facilitate popularity, leadership and interpersonal management.

As with other skills and abilities, some people will have stronger competencies than others. By understanding emotional intelligence, we become better able to strengthen those competencies we have not fully developed.

Gender Issues Associated with Emotional Intelligence

One idea addressed by Daniel Goleman is regarding gender issues. Although men and women may approach business in a slightly different way, the explosive growth of women-owned businesses over the past decade attests to the success of their non-traditional style.

"Men who are high in emotional intelligence are socially poised, outgoing and cheerful, not prone to fearfulness or worried rumination. They have a notable capacity for commitment to people or causes, for taking responsibility, and for having an ethical outlook; they are sympathetic and caring in their relationships.

Their emotional life is rich, but appropriate; they are comfortable with them-selves, others, and the social universe they live in."

By contrast, "emotionally intelligent women tend to be assertive and expres-sive about their feelings. They need to feel positive about themselves; life holds meaning for them. Like the men, they are outgoing and gregarious, and express their feelings appropriately; they adapt well to stress. Their social poise lets them easily reach out to new people; they are comfortable enough with themselves to be playful, spontaneous, and open to sensual experience. Unlike the women purely high in IQ, they rarely feel anxious and guilty, or sink into rumination."

As you can see, emotional intelligence is a different way of being smart. It includes knowing yourself and using your emotions to make good decisions; managing your feelings well; motivating yourself and others; maintaining hope in the face of adversity; exhibiting empathy; and managing relationships effectively. These skills matter significantly for your career and the workplace, for health and contentment.

Interests and Personality Traits

Starting a new business is risky even during times of economic prosperity. How-ever, the chances of succeeding will increase if you spend quality time evaluating yourself. Think about personal needs and circumstances and begin to anticipate and work out as many problems as you can *before* risking all of your assets.

Research shows it takes certain personality traits, which combine to form a specific character, to thrive in your own business, plus there are numerous skills and types of knowledge you will also need to acquire along the way. Besides tak-ing the self-assessment that follows, peruse the information under Appendix C. These will familiarize you with what is required. In addition, you may want to self-assess your attributes and your personal values and see how they compare to those of currently successful people. Do not forget to evaluate leadership and management skills and to polish the administrative skills as well.

Evaluate your qualifications as they pertain to each of the following state-ments:

    a.   **Organization and Planning:** time management, keeping work sched-ules, goal setting and goal achievement

    b.   **Managing Money:** creating budgets, securing loans, raising funds, maintaining financial records, controlling spending, and preparing IRS forms

c. **Sales and Marketing of Ideas and Products:** forecasting sales quotas and projections, presentation of products for organizations, potential clients, direct marketing to customers, ability to handle rejection and criticism

d. **Management:** experience with managing all or part of a small business, or your leadership role as an officer in an association

e. **Communication Skills and Working with People:** mediating with people with conflicting views when the need arises, event planning, handling complaints for an organization or corporation, ability to get along well with others

f. **Risk-Taker:** ability to handle calculated risks in different situations—situations where there was a reasonable chance of success

g. **Willingness to Lead and Work Alone:** ability to work and lead calmly and efficiently in the midst of an emergency or crisis

h. **Personality Traits:** being able to take the initiative in situations that require it, accepting and accomplishing more than your share of the work, being a hard worker despite no immediate financial rewards, ability to establish high standards of performance, and evaluating and raising the standards as needed

i. **Product Knowledge and/or Skills in the Service offered by the Company:** ability to learn quickly and without much supervision, willingness to research and plan in order to improve business operations.

Using your resumé or curriculum vitae complete the skills assessment that follows. Be honest with yourself in order pinpoint strengths as well as areas that may pose a challenge. First, answer YES or NO to the question (i.e. can I organize and plan?) If your answer is YES, then elaborate on your experience(s).

Skills Assessment

SKILL	Can I...?	Years of Experience	Was I in a leadership role?	Describe the Work
Organize & Plan				
Manage Money				
Sell & Market				
Manage People				
Communicate				
Take Risks				
Work Alone				
Lead the Team				
Train the Team				

Review Skills-Assessment

The skills assessment gave you the opportunity to look in the mirror and self-analyze. Now that you have had some time to think about your previous experiences, jobs, internships and skills, see if what is on your graph correlates with the areas discussed below. The goal is to maximize your strengths and find ways of turning your challenges into opportunities. This can include taking a course or finding a mentor willing to sit down with you to help you articulate your goals and ideas.

Organization and planning

This step will get you, the entrepreneur, from where you are to where you want to be. Entrepreneurs need to be able to set short-term and long-term goals, they must plan for the day, the week, the month and the year, yet maintain a level of flexibility which enables them to react to the many things that come up from minute to minute. Initially this is crucial, as the entrepreneur will be wearing many hats: employee, accountant, sales and marketing manager, and office manager. As the entrepreneur, you will need to explore various ways to maximize your time and energy in order for your business to grow. By setting S.M.A.R.T. goals, you will begin to pave the road.

S   **Specific** goals give a clear definition of where the entrepreneur is headed, what needs to be accomplished, how it will be accomplished and by whom.

M   **Measurable** goals provide the entrepreneur with more tangible evidence of completion. It will make you feel good to see what you have accomplished and will prove to you that your time was not wasted.

A   **Achievable** goals enable the entrepreneur to set the goal rather than have it set by someone else. You know your strengths and weaknesses best and can use this information to set goals you will be able to accomplish.

R   **Realistic** goals keep you on track and help you to plan things you are likely to follow through with. However, realistic is not a synonym for easy. It is better to set a few goals you know you can accomplish than to set many you will not be able to complete. Quality is better than quantity.

T   **Timeliness** of the goal is important. When do you plan to work towards your goal? If the goal will take you more than two hours to complete, break the task into manageable chunks. Time must be measurable, and tasks attainable and realistic.

Managing Money

Create a budget, secure financing and control spending to avoid over-extending. When dealing with finances, do not be wildly optimistic. A venture capitalist is looking for someone who has feet firmly on the ground. An entrepreneur needs a clear, logical business plan; one that is based on a good, old-fashioned business model. Keep to the basic rules of profitability. Does the business plan allow investors to see the essentials of the business, such as how revenues are generated, and the size of the market share, and is there an exit strategy so they can liquidate their investment? Do not overspend or get into too much debt. Do not imagine, or count on, money that is not there. Like the average homeowner, be aware of the approximate value of the business, examine what the competition is doing and, if needed, remodel the strategy. Finally, keep in mind that success does not happen overnight and some sacrifices will need to be made.

Sales and Marketing of Ideas

Entrepreneurs need to get customers in the door to sell products, BUT marketing is essential to get customers in. What a vicious circle! Before working on a marketing plan, check out what the competition is doing, find similar non-competing businesses and find out how they are getting their names out. If the business is starting from scratch, budget more for it. It takes more effort, and often more money, to make a name for a new business. Finally, review the plan periodically and adjust the expenditures as needed.

Managing

An entrepreneur planning to own a business must develop management skills. The growth of the business is tied to good management skills and practices. Entrepreneurs must have qualities that allow them to manage finance, budgets, personnel, and sales. Most importantly, they must be able to manage change because it is pervasive in business today. Strong change-management skills are essential for the business to be a success. Change-management skills include leadership development (to get people to believe in you), marketing and sales abilities (to promote your case for change), and communication skills (to help build support for the decision to change).

Communication Skills and Working with People

While the Golden Rule "do unto others as you would have them do unto you" may be evident in the way we conduct our personal lives, this axiom has taken on new importance as a policy in the world of business. Entrepreneurs must be able to communicate strategy and company goals to employees, and product value and service to their customers. They must be able to listen to constructive criticism and feedback. They must be able to provide a work environment that applauds success and at the same time is flexible enough to adjust, based on the market and competition.

Risk-Taker

True entrepreneurs are not necessarily foolish gamblers or risk-takers. They tend to be willing to take carefully calculated risks after careful thought and planning—thereby reducing the risk. This is better than dragging one's feet too long, wasting precious time in over-analyzing things. Rather than having a negative outlook, successful entrepreneurs have a "can do" attitude, and see opportunity where others only see problems. Needless to say, there is financial risk associated with starting a business. Until the business takes off, income may go up and down dramatically. In addition, one may have to invest personal savings and use personal assets as collateral for business loans.

Willingness to Lead and Work Alone

Many entrepreneurs choose not to have employees or associates on their payroll. Initially, most cannot afford to hire any help and opt to become the lone ranger instead. They control every event and perform all of the tasks required for the business. However, being the boss has its downside. The most frequently cited disadvantage is the long hard hours, particularly during the start-up period. It takes a great amount of effort to get a business up and running. That may mean working late into the night and every weekend for some time.

Personality Traits

Entrepreneurship is not just about having a lot of innovative ideas or knowledge regarding business. It is also about having a lot of guts. Studies have identified a variety of personality characteristics associated with successful entrepreneurs. Among the most important are a healthy sense of self-confidence and an optimistic attitude. Successful entrepreneurs take risks, but they are calculated risks. They do not plunge blindly into new situations. Instead, they are thorough and prepared. It does not take being a genius to be the best entrepreneur. The best and most successful entrepreneur is an expert in spotting great business opportunities. What is needed is the ability to be disciplined and focused.

It has been demonstrated that entrepreneurs are not just motivated by a desire to earn a living. They usually have an interest in their line of business and it rarely seems like work to them. It helps them put in the long hours getting a business up and running.

Product Knowledge and/or skills in the Service offered by the company

An entrepreneur needs to be able to market and sell the service or product being offered. The inability to answer a customer's questions may result in lack of trust in the service being provided or product being sold.

If any of these poses a weakness, develop a plan to acquire the necessary skills and experience. After giving the assessment more thought, complete the last column on the Skills Assessment chart that follows. Include information regarding the plan for improvement and the timeline in which it will be accomplished. This will help to outline a path and will get the wheels moving in the right direction. For example, if the answer to the question *Can I manage money?* is NO; the action plan could include taking a course on budgeting and money management at your local college within 30 days. The goal is to see each NO as an opportunity for professional development. The key is ensuring the amount of time given to complete the training is reasonable. Reasonable is usually within 30 days unless it is a three-month course offered during a reasonable timeframe.

Skills Assessment - Action Plan

SKILL	Can I...?	Years of Experience	Was I in a leadership role?	Describe the Work	Plan to Improve
Organize & Plan					
Manage Money					
Sell & Market					
Manage People					
Communicate					
Take Risks					
Work Alone					
Lead the Team					
Train the Team					

3

Start with Baby Steps

"The successful person makes a habit of doing what the failing person does not."

—*Thomas Edison, inventor and scientist*

Getting the Business Up and Running

Before building a viable business, learn the essential steps in getting a company up and running. The first step in starting a business is to identify an opportunity. Keep your eyes open; observe and listen; inquire; and, look for unmet needs you could address through a new product or service.

Conduct market research to determine the true potential for the idea. Do not jump into anything until the opportunity is real. Read everything available and talk with potential customers, as well as other professionals in the field. Ask the following questions:

- Is there a real market? Is it growing?

- How much are customers willing to pay for the product?

- Who is the competition? Is there a competitive advantage?

- What obstacles will have to be overcome?

- What resources are essential to enter the market?

Next, develop a business plan. The process of writing things down will help refine thinking and will focus your efforts. A good business plan contains the following components:

- Market analysis

- Mission statement, long term goals, and specific objectives
- Description of the product or service that is being offered
- Product development plan
- Marketing strategies
- Operations plan, covering details such as manufacturing and distribution
- Financial plan (including cash flow analysis).

One of the biggest challenges for a start-up business is obtaining adequate financing. Among the possible sources of funding are savings, friends and family, lending institutions and venture capitalists. However, all come with a cost. For example, personal assets may have to be used as collateral for a loan and future profits are jeopardized when investors are brought in. Consider the long-term impact of the alternatives before making any decisions.

Before the grand opening, the legal status of the business must be established. Options include: sole proprietorship, partnership, limited partnership and corporation.

Sole proprietorship

Under the title sole proprietorship, the owner IS the business. All profits and losses come from the individual. Sole proprietorships are owned and operated by one person and that person has unlimited personal liability. This means that if anything happens and you file for bankruptcy, the IRS, in the event of a tax liability, can claim anything and everything you have, regardless of whether or not it belonged to the business. Despite this, it is the most widely used business structure. It does have its advantages and disadvantages. The greatest advantage is that it is easy to form and has the least amount of government intervention. This allows you to be very flexible and have complete responsibility and control of the business. As for taxes, all income and losses are consolidated on your personal income tax return. Sound great, huh? The disadvantages are just as numerous. As stated before, the owner has unlimited personal liability, meaning that personal property can be constrained to settle debts with creditors. With a sole proprietorship the business ends if the owner quits, because the owner IS the business. You have complete responsibility and control of the business; if something goes wrong, it is completely your fault. The last two disadvantages are that you may have a limited ability to raise capital and fewer resources and talents to draw from.

Partnership

A partnership is a voluntary association of two or more individuals who act as co-owners of the business. Their talents are combined to run the company, and partnerships always have an agreement drawn up that spells out the rights and duties of all the partners (and their descendants) to help avoid legal disputes later on in the life of the business. As with the sole proprietorship, partnerships are flexible and easy to form. They have limited government intervention and there may be possible tax advantages since your income is taxed as personal income. The greatest benefit is that you have several individuals from whom to draw ideas and funding opportunities. The disadvantages are less concrete, the main one being that at least one partner has unlimited personal liability. A partnership may also make it harder to get large sums of money. The ethical and legal dilemma: the actions of one partner can make the entire business liable.

Corporation

A corporation is entirely different from a sole proprietorship or a partnership in that it becomes a separate entity formed by filing Articles of Incorporation with your Secretary of State. Business taxes are filed separate from the owners because the owner and the business are legally separate. There are two types, an S corporation and a Limited Liability Corporation. Each has the same advantages, limited personal liability, ownership can be transferred through stock sales and the business has unlimited life. With a corporation, it is easier to obtain money and it gives an impression of credibility to potential and current customers. However, there are some disadvantages. Business activity may be restricted by the charter; extensive record keeping may be required; and, double taxation.

The "double taxation" of dividends is often cited as one of the disadvantages of the corporate form of business organization. The way corporations are taxed provides some interesting and challenging planning decisions. A corporation is a taxpaying entity. That is, it must file an annual tax return and pay taxes on its income. If those earnings are distributed to a shareholder, this distribution is treated as a *dividend*, which is then taxable to the shareholder. The effect of this is that corporate earnings are taxed twice—once at the corporate level and once at the shareholder level, when the earnings are distributed in the form of dividends.

The second method for eliminating double taxation is the use of a device called an *S Corporation*. This is a type of corporation specifically provided for in the Internal Revenue Code. An S Corporation is treated differently for tax purposes than a conventional corporation (which is known as a "C Corporation"). If elected by the shareholders, an S Corporation will not be subject to tax at the corporate level. Instead, all corporate income is included directly in the income of the shareholders. There is no need to zero out the corporation with salaries since corporate income is now subject to tax only once, at the shareholder level. Additionally, if the corporation has a *net loss*, that loss can be used by the shareholders to offset other business income.

In order to qualify, the stock of an S Corporation must be held by 75 or fewer individuals and all shareholders must consent to the election. An S Corporation has all of the lawsuit protection features of a C Corporation. If unreasonable compensation is an issue or the corporation is expected to show net losses, an S Corporation would be a useful planning technique.

The two types of corporations have specific advantages as well. Under an S Corporation, you continue to have limited personal liability but if there is more than one owner then it becomes more expensive to form than if a sole proprietorship or partnership is formed. The limited liability corporation also has limited personal liability and can include more than 35 shareholders, but it becomes more expensive to form if there is to be more than one owner.

Family-owned businesses

These have additional challenges above and beyond managing a small business because the owner(s) and worker(s) need to be able to separate family and business issues during the business day. Family-owned businesses have the potential to earn great amounts of money and are flexible and stable because of the support of family, but it is not always that great. The disadvantages include: family and non-family management disputes; and problems regarding succession.

Home-based businesses

Much like the family-owned business, the only major difference is that the business is located in your home. The determining factor of opening a home-based business is that a new physical location is not needed. The advantages of home-based businesses are the low overhead cost and the flexibility to allow you to work at any time of the day. Some disadvantages include feeling isolated or lacking the discipline needed to conduct business from home. However, it is very important that you check the zoning laws to be sure you can operate your business out of your home. You need to have self-discipline, a clean workspace, technological support, and patience.

You may also need certain licenses to operate the business. The Small Business Association or an attorney can clarify any questions regarding these legal issues.

There are countless decisions to make as the opening gets closer: what equipment to buy, where to locate the office, what business stationery to use, what policies and procedures to implement, and more. Take time and think through the alternatives before making potentially costly choices.

During the start-up phase, avoid hiring any full-time employees. Consider using outside contractors to help with the initial set-up. When the time comes to start hiring, think carefully. Who will work for the business? Build a team that will really make a contribution.

It is crucial to set up a good accounting system. There are revenues and expenses to track, cash flow to manage, and taxes to plan for. Find someone to advise on the information needed and the best way to manage it.

Are you Chasing Rainbows?

Before starting a business, think about the business idea or concept in the light of your knowledge, education, and abilities as well as in the context of market needs. This is how you go from idea to implementation. Before you begin to develop your business idea, you need to determine its strength and viability.

What type of business should you start? Should you start a business by developing a business idea in an area in which you already have the expertise or by exploring a new direction in which you develop an idea or concept?

Regardless of whether you start a business in an area in which you already have experience, or start with a completely new concept, you will want to validate your idea.

Being a successful entrepreneur, creating an innovative new product, bringing it to market, and making a profit, is a dream that many of us share. You have looked in the mirror and determined that you have the necessary skills, drive and motivation to start your own business. You are willing to put everything at risk and pour your heart and soul into your new business venture. So now you are ready to evaluate your idea. Evaluating new business ideas is an essential skill for any would-be entrepreneur. Here are a few important things to do when evaluating new business ideas:

Think and Rethink

Introducing new products or services without evaluating the market is like skydiving without a parachute. In fact, many businesses fail because there is no adequate market for their products or services. Before risking assets and resources on the product or service, it is essential to obtain a clear picture of the market being targeted. While ascertaining the customer's reaction to a new product is difficult, as an entrepreneur you can get information on the market by conducting formal market research. Does the idea fill a need or create one? Who is buying it? Why are they buying? Is it difficult to manufacture? Are any competitors developing a similar product?

Two brains are better than one

Get friends, colleagues or acquaintances who are particularly smart, to provide feedback on the idea. Look for other entrepreneurs who have a record of success—prior entrepreneurs and venture capitalists are perfect. Have a brainstorming session to discuss how the target market might receive the idea and what possible points will pose a challenge. Be objective! Be impartial! Listen!

Customer knows best

Entrepreneurs are so attached to their ideas that they forget to focus on the needs of their potential customers. However, no idea will succeed without a customer. Find a customer and ask him or her the obvious questions: Do you like the idea? Would you purchase it? How much are you willing to pay for it? Do you think there is a problem with what I am trying to sell? Have you seen another product like this one? If I build it, will you be my guinea pig and test it?

Sleep, Think, Rethink, Sleep

Do not quit the day job. Take time to evaluate the entrepreneurial concept. A great idea may stay as an idea after it is thought through, or it can be transformed into greatness. Think about it for a few weeks and see if after that time you are still excited about the idea.

Outline your Business Plan

If you have talked about it with others, researched customer interest, and thought it through for a while, and still feel it is a good idea, then it is best to quickly outline the business plan. Begin with writing a description of the product or service. Itemize costs and projected revenues. Identify the risks and challenges. Think about building a team. Analyze how you will handle competitive threats.

This evaluative phase will provide useful feedback regarding the product's uniqueness and appeal, the competition, the growth potential and the marketing route to explore. Now you are ready to GO FOR IT! Life is too short to let good ideas waste away. Even if you fail, you will have fun trying. And, in any case, next time around you will be much better at evaluating new business ideas!

Power of Market Research

One crucial problem you will face after expressing an interest in starting a business will be determining the feasibility of your idea. Market Research is an important step in this process.

Market Research is the systematic and objective collection of data about the target market. It also looks at the competition and environment with the goal of increased understanding regarding demographics and market needs. The data collected should be used to guide important strategic business decisions.

Furthermore, Market Research maps the communication with current and potential customers. It helps identify opportunities in the market place and minimizes the risk of doing business. Market research also uncovers and identifies potential problems or challenges, and creates benchmarks. It helps track progress and evaluates success.

According to the National Women's Business Center (July 1997) well-conducted Market Research provides information regarding market segmentation, purchasing power and buying habits, psychological aspects of the market, market-place competition, and environmental factors.

Market segmentation

What characteristics do the customers share? Who are the customers? What is the size of their population? What is the gender breakdown (i.e. percentage male, female)? What are their ages, races, incomes and education levels? What are their occupations, skills, interests and hobbies? How many children do they have? Do they have pets? Where do they live and work?

Purchasing-power and buying habits

What financial strength and economic attributes does the target market have? What is the average dollar amount spent on purchases or products or services similar to mine? What are the financing needs of the target market? What is their current usage of services? When do they purchase? Where do they shop? Why do they buy? How often do they purchase? How much do they buy at a time? Do they own or rent their homes? What types of cars do they drive? How often do they eat out? How do they typically spend their disposable income? What methods of payment do they use? How strong is their credit?

Psychological aspects of the market

What are the values and opinions shared by the consumers in the market? What is the reaction of the market to the products or services? How does the market compare my company to other businesses? What qualities and characteristics do the customers deem important? Who makes the decision to buy? What are the deciding factors in making a purchase? Do they only want the best for their family? Are they looking for convenience and time-saving devices? Are they concerned with how they are perceived by others? What are their unmet needs? Do they demand intensive customer service? Are they only concerned with the lowest price? What media (magazines, radio, TV, newspapers, Internet providers, etc.) are they exposed to? What confuses the customers and prospects?

Marketplace competition

What do I know about the other companies within the area of business? Who are the main competitors? How do they compete with me? In what ways do they not compete with me? What are their strengths and weaknesses? Are there profitable opportunities based upon their weaknesses? What is their market niche? What makes this business unique from the others? How do competitors position themselves? How do they communicate their services? Who are their customers? How are they perceived by the market? Who are the industry leaders? What is their sales volume? Where are they located? Are they profitable?

Environmental factors

What are the factors that can influence productivity and operations? What are the current and future population trends? What are the current and future socio-economic trends? What effects do economic and political policies have on the target market or my industry? What are the growth expectations for the market? What outside factors influence the industry's performance? What are the trends for this market and for the economy? Is the industry growing, at a plateau, or declining?

Successful small businesses have knowledge about all of these issues. Acquiring accurate and specific information is a critical step in market analysis and the development of a market plan. The primary focus is to:

- Understand the customers' need

- Develop a product or service that will meet that customer need

- Create promotional material that will make the customer aware

- Ensure product or service delivery

Upon evaluating what the Market Research is saying, it is time to create a marketing plan. The most difficult part about writing a plan is that there are no easy rules to follow! Marketing plans vary. The components will be different depending on the industry, the size of company, and its stage of growth. The *format* is not as important as the process of preparing it. And that *process* will make you think about your goals and the marketing strategy required to achieve them.

Below is an outline of a typical marketing plan. You may use this model to help brainstorm and generate ideas. The marketing plan may contain all of these components or just a few, depending on the company type, stage of growth, and goals.

Sample Marketing Plan

Executive Summary

In the Executive Summary you introduce the company and provide a brief explanation of the plan.

- Description of the company

- Products and services offered

- Company mission statement

- Goals and objectives of the company

- Organization Chart, including management and marketing teams

- A summary of the marketing goals and recommended strategies based on your Market Research

- Business form: proprietorship, partnership, or corporation?

- Type of business: merchandising, manufacturing, or service?

- What is the product or service?

- Is it a new business? A takeover? An expansion?

- Why will this business be profitable?

- When will the business open?

- Is it a seasonal business?

- What have you learned about the business from outside sources (trade suppliers, bankers, other business owners, publications)?

Current Situation

In this section, provide information regarding the locale, target market and competitive environment. In addition, point out any important problems the company may face.

- Provide a thorough description of your location including both current location and future location (if applicable).

- Describe your target market. What are the demographics? This includes characteristics of the population that influence consumption of products and services. They include age, sex, race, family size, level of education, occupation, income and location of residence.

- Include a brief analysis of your competitors.

Competition and Problem Analysis

Elaborate on what you briefly mentioned in the competitor's analysis in the previous section.

- Who offers similar products or services?

- How does the product or service stand against theirs?

- List any important business problems that are potential challenges (i.e. new ordinances or a prospective technological advance that may replace the product or service).

Marketing Objectives

State your marketing objectives.

- How will awareness of your product be increased among target consumers?

- What is the timeframe for achieving the objectives?

Marketing Strategy

Here is the blueprint! This is how you plan to achieve marketing objectives. Follow the 4Ps of marketing.

Product

Describe the product or service in detail. What are the product's features and benefits?

Price

What is your strategy for setting the price of the product or service, and what are the payment methods?

Promotion

Describe the promotional plan (i.e. telemarketing, direct mail, or flyers). What promotional tool(s) will be used to accomplish the marketing objectives?

Place

Where will the product be displayed so customers have access to it, and how will you make the sales? What is the sales and distribution strategy?

Action Programs

Create a marketing "to do" list. Provide a synopsis of what will be done, when it will begin, date for completion, and who is responsible.

Budget

List the cost of the marketing activities described in the marketing plan. How will marketing be paid for?

Measurements

Have quantifiable objectives that will measure the results of implementing the marketing plan. Include time limits for achieving the goals. For example, increase sales by 5 percent in 6 months.

Supporting Documents

Include supporting documents as needed to cover the areas included in the marketing plan. These may include résumes of important management personnel, budgets, market research results, etc.

4

Building the Foundation

"Those who enter to buy, support me. Those who come to flatter, please me. Those who complain, teach me how I may please others so that more will come. Only those hurt me who are displeased but do not complain. They refuse me permission to correct my errors."

—Marshall Field, entrepreneur

Do I need a business plan?

You have thought about this since the day you dreamt of opening a lemonade stand: the day when the brilliant idea would yield both financial and emotional rewards. Now that you are an adult, you are ready to embark on the enterprise journey. At this point, the four core questions have been answered and you are ready to write the business plan. You have pinpointed the service or product your business will provide; you know who the potential customers for your product are; you have an idea of how you will reach your customers; and you have researched the financial resources that will help you start your business.

Just as a conductor does not begin a concert without the score, eager business owners should not rush into new ventures without a business plan. A business plan precisely defines your business, identifies your goals, and serves as the résumé for your company. The basic components include a current and pro forma balance sheet, an income statement, and a cash flow analysis. The business plan will enable you to allocate the resources appropriately, handle unforeseen challenges, and make solid business decisions. Because it provides organized information about the company and how borrowed money will be repaid, a good business plan is an integral part of any loan application. In addition, it informs sales personnel, suppliers, and others about the operations and goals.

A business plan is the blueprint of the company. It provides a strategic vision for the company; it becomes the most important piece of communication; it facilitates obtaining capital or loans; it is a tool for goal-setting and for evaluating and improving performance; it assists you when making decisions; and, it provides employees with direction.

You may have asked yourself, why should I spend my time and energy drawing this blueprint? The answer is simple. Lack of planning leaves you poorly equipped to anticipate future decisions and actions you must make or take to run your business successfully. On the other hand, a sound plan can act as a:

Reality check

The process of putting a business plan together, including the thought put in before it is written, forces you to take an objective, critical, unemotional look at the business project in its entirety.

Evaluative tool

The written business plan is an operating tool. It allows you to set realistic goals and objectives for the company's performance, and, if maintained, will also provide a basis for evaluating and controlling the company's performance in the future.

Message sender

The completed business plan communicates the company's ideas and message to employees, outside directors, lenders, and potential investors outside the company. A business plan helps do that in an organized, credible manner. Also, the process of planning helps determine if the vision is realistic, and tells you what needs to be done in order to achieve it.

Motivation tool

The development of the business plan is one of the best ways to communicate how well you understand the business and describe the vision of the business. Without proper planning, it becomes impossible to get all of the employees reading off the same page of the book and generating energy through high levels of teamwork. It is impossible to motivate people when they do not know where they are going or what they are trying to achieve.

Management development tool

Putting together the business plan will help you develop as a manager because it provides practice in thinking and figuring out problems about competitive conditions, promotional opportunities, and situations that are or may be beneficial or harmful to the business.

Road map

The business plan, once it is completed, will give you and the employees goals and direction: a roadmap to follow in guiding the business through good and bad times.

Overall, a business plan must provide three things. These are:

- **Evidence of focus.** What do we do exceptionally well?

- **Understanding of who the target customers are.** Provide a clear definition of the target customer

- **An appreciation of investor or lender needs.** How can I foster a mutually beneficial relationship? What are the needs of the investor or lender?

Starting the Business Planning Process

Before writing the business plan, a few things need to be put in perspective. These include: identifying the vision; seeking support; and, evaluating whether the vision is feasible by conducting a SWOT analysis (Strengths, Weaknesses, Opportunities, and Threats) and a MECA assessment (Market, Environmental, and Competitive Assessment).

Identify your vision and imagineer it

Imagineering simply means using your imagination to engineer (i.e. plan) achieving the goals. Describe the vision for the company. Is it to develop a state-of-the-art product? Perhaps it is as simple as gaining financial independence or paying for your children's education. Let your imagination run free. However, once the vision is defined, stand on level ground and develop a plan. Set measurable goals and objectives. Do not forget to brainstorm to generate different and creative ideas to achieve those goals.

Seek support

Whether starting a business or expanding one, hard work is always on the horizon. Support from family or colleagues will make the days a little easier. Find people who will embrace the vision, those who will stand by it during tough times.

Is the vision feasible?

Conducting a SWOT analysis will facilitate evaluation of the business's strengths, weaknesses, opportunities and threats as well as your own. SWOT is a business tool that helps determine whether the vision in mind is feasible.

There are four steps in the SWOT analysis:

S   Strengths
Identify the strengths. Consider: ability and potential, persistence, confidence, innovation, sales experience, track record, financial stability, and expertise.

W   Weaknesses
Identify the weaknesses. What are the weaknesses? Consider: lack of time, health, financial instability, lack of family support, no management experience, lack of social skills, and others.

O   Opportunities
Identify the opportunities. What opportunities exist? Consider: connections with a successful entrepreneur, work in a related field, business development assistance, supportive network, and community resources.

T   Threats
Identify the threats. What are the threats? Consider the following: personal or family issues, instability of market, a financial crisis, loss of job, health concerns, and others.

After you have completed your personal SWOT analysis, complete one for the business. To determine the business's strengths, weaknesses, opportunities, and threats, it is important to gather information from outside of the business. This is where a MECA (Market, Environmental, and Competitive Assessment) comes into play. A MECA will provide data for the business's SWOT analysis while, at the same time, providing valuable information for developing the strategic plan. Think of a MECA as the *big picture* analysis. During this process look for trends, voids, and opportunities related to the market and the competition. According to the National Association of Women Business Owners (May 1997) these are some things to keep in mind when conducting the MECA:

Make a few assumptions

Although it is impossible to predict the future, it is important to make some assumptions related to the future performance of the business. This is the only way to persuade others to become involved in the business—especially if you are asking for capital. State the assumptions clearly. Researching the market will help recognize trends and identify industry norms. The important thing is to make sure the reader is not left guessing since most lenders will assume the worst if given the opportunity.

Develop operating plans

Include key risk assessment. What happens if…? How will the goals be reached? What is needed in order to produce or sell? How much? At what price? Who are the clients? Where are they? How are they reached? How much competition exists, and how will you compete successfully?

Develop financials

Financials include the balance sheet, income and cash flow statements. To prepare or update these, ask questions like: What are the day-to-day and month-to-month costs of running the business? What is the business's "break-even" point? Do I have the capital required for the business or will I have to raise it? Can I get it from friends and relatives? Will I have to go to a bank, or will I have the type of business that appeals to a venture capitalist?

Communicate, communicate, communicate

The business plan is an invaluable communication tool. It facilitates communication with others outside of the company and convinces them that the dream is realistic and that the idea can be implemented. It also provides focus and direction for employees, since everyone knows what the goals and objectives are and how they tie in to the big picture.

When the cycle begins again

Constantly revisit and revise the business plan to see how the business is performing. Ask yourself: How did I do? Did I walk the talk? How am I doing with achieving the goals and objectives? On an annual basis, reassess the entire plan to see if the business is performing as it was intended to.

Business Plan 101

When entrepreneurs hear the term business plan, they envision a one-inch thick document packed with every possible piece of business-related information. This is not always the case. A business plan can help you move forward, make decisions, and make the business successful. Not all business plans are the same, not every business needs the same level of detail. Develop a simple plan first as you start a small business, and that might be enough. In other words, start simple and then elaborate as you prepare to approach bankers or investors.

A business plan can also help to attract key employees, find new business prospects, manage the business more efficiently, as well as:

- Identify if there is a market for the product or service

- Determine the competition and identify advantages

- Estimate start-up costs, revenues, expenses, and profitability

- Shows if the business idea is worth pursuing

A business plan should include all the important matters that will contribute to making the business idea a success. Since business plans vary greatly in length and detail, the amount and type of information contained in a business plan also varies. The business plan should contain just enough information to accomplish its goal. No more. No less. Business plans are often 15 to 20 pages in length, but the plan may be shorter or longer.

One suggestion for getting started is to develop the plan in stages that meet that real business needs. Below is an outline of a business plan. Remember: initially, not all sections may be necessary.

Part 1: Business Information

A. Cover Sheet (Title Page)
Name, address, and telephone number of the company
Name, title, address, and telephone number of owners/corporate officers
Month and year your plan was prepared
Name of the person preparing the plan
Copy number of the plan

B. Executive Summary (Statement of Purpose)
The statement of purpose states the business plan objectives

Summarize the following:
Company (who, what, where, when)
Who is the management? What are their strengths?
What are the objectives? Why will the business be successful?
If the business needs financing, why does it need it? How much is needed? How will the business repay the loan or benefit the investor?

TIP: Do not write the Executive Summary until the business plan is complete! It should reflect the contents of the finished plan.

C. Table of Contents (Refer to the major areas of your plan)

Part 2: Organizational Plan

A. Summary Description of the Business
In a few paragraphs, give a broad overview of the nature of the business, telling when and why the company was formed. Then complete the summary by briefly addressing:

- Mission (projecting short- and long-term goals)

- Business Model (describe the company's model and why it is unique to the industry)

- Strategy (give an overview of the strategy, focusing on short- and long-term objectives)

- Strategic Relationships (tell about any existing strategic relationships)

- Risks (that the company will face, both external and internal)

B. Products or Services

- If the business is the manufacturer and/or wholesale distributor of a product: Describe the products. Tell briefly about the manufacturing process. Include information on suppliers and availability of materials.

- If the business is a retailer and/or an e-tailer: Describe the products the business sells. Include information about the sources and handling of inventory and fulfillment.

- If the business provides a service: Describe the services; List future products or services the business plans to provide.

C. Intellectual Property
Address Copyrights, Trademarks, and Patents
Include Supporting Documents such as registrations, photos, and diagrams
The supporting documents should include all of the documents the business completed to incorporate or to officially open the business.

D. Location
Describe the projected or current location
Project costs associated with the location
Have legal agreements, utility forecasts, and other supporting documents in case they are needed for financial reasons.

E. Legal Structure
Describe the legal structure and why it is advantageous for the company
List owners and/or corporate officers describing strengths (include resumés)

F. Management
List the people who are (or will be) running the business
Describe their responsibilities and abilities
Project their salaries

G. Personnel
How many employees will the business have? What positions?
What are the necessary qualifications?
How many hours will they work and at what salary?
Project future needs for adding employees

H. Accounting and Legal
Accounting: what systems will the business set up for daily accounting? Who will the business use as a tax accountant? Who will be responsible for periodic financial statement analysis?
Legal: Will the business retain an attorney?

I. Insurance
What kind of insurance will the business carry? (Property & Liability, Life & Health)
What will it cost? Who will the business use as the insurance carrier?

J. Security

Address security in terms of inventory control and theft of information (online and off).

Project related costs

Part 3: The Marketing Plan

The Marketing Plan defines all of the components of the business marketing strategy. It will address the details of the market analysis, sales, advertising, and public relations campaigns. The Plan should also integrate traditional (offline) programs with new media (online) strategies.

A. Overview and goals of the marketing strategy

B. Market Analysis

- Target Market (identify with demographics, psychographics, and niche market specifics)

- Competition (describe major competitors, assessing their strengths and weaknesses

- Market Trends (identify industry trends and customer trends)

- Market Research (describe methods of research, database analysis, and results summary)

C. Marketing Strategy and Implementation Plan

- General Description (Budget allocations with expected ROIs)

- Method of Sales and Distribution (stores, offices, kiosks, catalogs, e-mail, website)

- Packaging, Pricing and Branding

- Database Marketing (Personalization)

- Sales Strategies (direct sales, direct mail, email, affiliate, reciprocal, and viral marketing)

- Sales Incentives/Promotions (samples, coupons, online promo, add-ons, rebates, etc.)

- Advertising Strategies (traditional, web/new media, long-term sponsorships)

- Public Relations (online presence, events, press releases, interviews)

- Networking (memberships and leadership positions)

- Customer Service (activities and expected outcomes)

- Implementation responsibilities (in-house and outside)

D. Assessment of Marketing Effectiveness
* This will need to be developed once the company evaluates the business, usually after the first year and each year after that.

Part 4: Financial Documents

Most entrepreneurs experience little difficulty when it comes to writing the text portion of the business plan, but when it comes to the financial portion of the business plan, many get stuck. To make this task easier, think of this section as the quantitative interpretation of everything stated in the organizational and marketing plans. Do not do this part of the plan until those two sections have been completed.

Financial documents are the records used to show past, current, and projected finances. Following are the major documents the business will want to include in the Business Plan. The work is much easier if they are done in the order presented because they build on each other, using information from the ones previously developed.

A. Summary of Financial Needs
(This section is used when approaching investors or banks for financing)
(1) Why the business is seeking financing
(2) How much capital will the business need?

B. Loan Fund Dispersal Statement
(This section is used when approaching investors or banks for financing)
In this section answer the following question, how does the business intend to disperse the loan funds? Include in this section supporting data, use charts and graphs if possible.

C. Projected Cash Flow Statement (Projected Budget)

This statement projects what the Business Plan means in terms of dollars. It shows cash inflow and outflow over a period and is used for internal planning. It is of prime interest to the lender and shows how the business intends to repay the loan. Cash flow statements show both how much and when cash must flow in and out of the business.

D. Three-Year Income Projection

A Profit and Loss Statement (Income Statement) shows the projections for the company for the next three years. Use the revenue and expense totals from the Cash Flow Statement for the first year's figures and project for the next two years according to expected economic and industry trends.

E. Projected Balance Sheet

Projection of Assets, Liabilities, and Net Worth of the company at end of the fiscal year.

F. Break-Even Analysis

The break-even point is the point at which a company's expenses exactly match the sales or service volume. It can be expressed in (1) Total dollars or revenue exactly offset by total expenses, or (2) Total units of production (cost of which exactly equals the income derived from their sales). This analysis can be done either mathematically or graphically. Revenue and expense figures are drawn from the three-year income projection.

If the business is new and has not yet begun operations, the financial section will end here and the business will add a Personal Financial History as section G. If not, continue with the following performance statements.

G. Income Statement

Shows the business financial activity over a period (monthly, annually). It is a living document showing what has happened in the business and is an excellent tool for assessing the business. The ledger is closed and balanced and the revenue and expense totals transferred to this statement.

H. Balance Sheet

Shows the condition of the business as of a fixed date. It is a picture of the firm's financial condition at a particular moment and will show whether the financial position of the business is strong or weak. It is usually done at the close of an accounting period and includes (1) Assets, (2) Liabilities and (3) Net Worth.

I. Financial Statement Analysis

In this section use the income statements and balance sheets to develop a study of relationships and comparisons of (1) Items in a single year's financial statement, (2) comparative financial statements for a period, or (3) the business statements with those of other businesses. Measures are expressed as ratios or percentages that can be used to compare the business with industry standards.

- Liquidity Analysis (net working capital, current ratio, quick ratio)
- Profitability Analysis (gross profit margin, operating profit margin, net profit margin)
- Debt Ratios (debt to assets, debt to equity)
- Measures of Investment (return on investment)
- Vertical financial statement analysis (shows relationship of components in a single financial statement)
- Horizontal financial statement analysis (percentage analysis of the increases and decreases in the items on comparative financial statement)

J. Business Financial History

This is a summary of financial information about the company from its start to the present. The Business Financial History and Loan Application are frequently the same. If the business has completed the rest of the financial section, the business should have all of the information needed to transfer to this document.

Part 5: Supporting Documents

This section will contain all of the records that back up the statements and decisions made in the four main parts of the business plan. The most common supporting documents are:

A. Resumés (owners and management)

B. Owner's Financial Statements (Statement of personal assets and liabilities. For a new business owner this will be part of the financial section as Section G in Part 4)

C. Credit Reports
D. Contracts, Leases and Agreements
E. Letters of Reference
G. Other Legal Documents (proprietary rights, insurance, limited partnership agreements, shipping contracts, etc)
H. Miscellaneous Documents (location plans, demographics, competition analysis, advertising rate sheets, cost analysis, etc.)

Ultimately, the choice of plan is based on the type of business, financing requirements and business objectives. The business plan takes precedence over purchasing business stationery, telephones, or finding a location.

Marketing

According to the American Marketing Association, *marketing* is:

The process of planning and executing the conception, pricing, promotion and distribution of ideas, goods, and services to create exchanges that satisfy individual and organizational objectives.

This definition implies that the process of marketing begins with determining what product(s) customers want to purchase. Providing the features and the quality customers want is a *crucial* first step in marketing. Otherwise the business will be rowing upstream by providing something *you want to produce* and then trying to *convince* someone to buy it.

The marketing process then continues with setting a price, letting potential customers know about the product or service, and making it available to them. Marketing is about answering four key questions:

WHAT?

What is the business going to sell (in exact detail)? How will it be packaged, and what services will be provided with it? And what price will the business charge for it?

WHO?

Who is the business going to sell to (in exact detail)? Will it be to other businesses, to private individuals, or who?

WHERE?

Where is the business going to make the sale? For instance, will the business sell over the Internet, from a shop, or by visiting customers' homes or businesses?

HOW?

How is the business going to promote the products and services?

Once these questions have been answered, the business is in a position to begin maximizing every opportunity to promote the products or services. Surprisingly, that does not imply costly advertising campaigns and elaborate promotional programs. According to Gwen Moran in *Promoting for Pennies* (Feb. 1994), many startup business owners overlook simple, inexpensive opportunities to promote themselves, create name recognition and increase sales through methods they already have in place. These opportunities cost far less than most traditional marketing methods and have been very effective for many entrepreneurs. Moran's suggestions include:

Invoices

When the business is preparing to mail the invoices, take this opportunity to stuff a flyer in the envelope highlighting any new products or services, and include a coupon for the products/services the business is promoting. If the business uses electronic invoices, take the time to include a link to the website or a blurb that will capture the client's attention.

On-hold programming

Who says the callers need to listen to elevator music? Instead of music, have customers on hold listen to latest product updates or promotions.

Cash register receipts

Have upcoming promotions, coupons or event information printed on the register receipts your customers receive.

E-Mail Signature

Besides the business name, include the contact information and the website with a hyperlink to the page highlighting the products and services. The business may also want to include dates for upcoming events.

Voice-Mail Messages

Do not leave a message stating that you are out of the office. Instead, invite callers to visit the website for the latest news and information regarding products or services.

Phone Manner and Customer Service

Make sure the frontline employees are courteous, friendly and informed. Receptionists gives the first impression of the company whether on the telephone or in person. Ensure that they are trained to provide the best perception of the company.

Labels

Create labels or stickers "Customer satisfaction is our goal", "If you love our products tell a friend", and paste them on outgoing correspondence.

Loyalty Rewards

A way to reward frequent shoppers with special coupons or gift certificates for additional product purchases. Keep them coming back!

Shipments

As the business prepares products for shipment, do not forget to include a catalog, flyer, coupons or an invitation to an upcoming event. The extra shipping cost is worth it!

Special postcards

Invest in sending birthday cards and holiday cards. It is a great way to personalize the services and to let the customers know that the business is celebrating with them.

5

Being the Big Boss Stinks!

o o o o o o o o o o o o o o o o o o o o o o o o o o o o o o o o o

"A code of ethics gives the people in a company a structure within which to make decisions."

—*David Thorpe, founder, Boston Knish Inc.*

Organizational Culture

Research suggests that culture is to an organization what personality is to an individual. As with personality, change takes time and may be difficult to communicate, especially for those inside the organization. For whose benefit does the organization exist? What are the basic assumptions among people who work in the organization? What are the basic assumptions the organization and the employee make in relation to each other?

"Culture" is omnipresent and is difficult to observe in various situations. It is everywhere and encompasses every aspect of our existence. Schein *(1992)* offers at least a partial solution in helping us to analyze organizational culture. He divides organizational culture into three levels:

1.   At the surface are *artifacts*, those aspects (such as dress) which can be easily discerned, yet are hard to understand;

2.   Beneath artifacts are *espoused values* which are conscious strategies, goals and philosophies; and,

3.   The core, or essence, of culture is represented by the basic underlying assumptions and values, which are difficult to detect because they exist at a largely unconscious level, yet provide the key to understanding why things happen the way they do.

Therefore, organizational culture may be described as the shared assumptions, beliefs, and norms (normal behaviors) of a group. These are powerful influences on the way people live and act, and they define what is *normal* and filter those who are not *normal*. To a large degree, our culture determines most of what we do.

Basically, organizational culture is the personality of the organization. Members of the organization can feel the particular culture that predominates. *Culture* is one of those concepts difficult to define clearly, yet everyone knows it when they sense it. For example, the culture of a large, for-profit corporation is quite different from a social service agency or hospital, which in turn is different from a university or college. You can get a better understanding of the culture of an organization by looking at the arrangement of offices, types of furnishings, what they brag about, what they are proud of, what members wear, what they spend money on, and how they treat their employees. This is very similar to getting a feeling about someone's personality.

So, what is the type of organizational culture that enhances the entrepreneurial spirit? Which work environment will quench the entrepreneur's thirst? The answers may vary. However, an environment that welcomes creativity and applauds innovation provides a start.

Innovation plays an essential role in industry and in people's lives. It proposes the idea that organizational culture, the *culture* of the workplace, should evolve in such a way that innovation becomes a part of the members' belief system. By weaving the spirit of innovation into the organizational culture, it is suggested that individuals within the organization will keep the business ideas fresh, flowing and ever-evolving. Small-business entrepreneurs, who can be more flexible than large corporations in their hiring practices and operations, are crucial in the process of building the foundation for the culture of innovation and fostering its growth. Consequently, successful entrepreneurs create cultures that have meaning for the employees. The meaning is a reflection of the entrepreneur's system of values and beliefs. For example, an entrepreneur who values family may be more open to providing flextime or the opportunity for employees to telecommute.

How does one analyze the culture that is predominant in an organization? Would one know where to start? What factors could affect the way the organization's culture is viewed? For some, looking at the age, gender, marital status, educational level and ethnicity of the employees will definitely provide insight into the organization's personality.

Age

Age simply does not matter any more. During the 1950s, 60s and 70s the large majority of people starting companies were in their 30s and 40s. Not true during the 1980s or today, Steve Jobs and Steve Wozniak were both in their early 20s when they started Apple Computer. At the other extreme, Ray Kroc was 59 when he started the McDonald's restaurant chain. For the individual with the entrepreneurial drive, age is not an obstacle. A Small Business Administration (SBA) study released in 2000, *The Third Millennium: Small Business and Entrepreneurship in the 21st Century*, notes that the average age of a worker will have increased from 35.9 years in 1988 to 40.7 years in 2008. What's more, corporate downsizing over the past 20 years has pushed many mid-career workers out of corporate jobs, enlarging the pool of older potential entrepreneurs. The SBA believes that, between 1996 and 2006, the number of self-employed workers will have grown by 50 percent, in part because of these older entrepreneurs. This growth probably will occur whether the American economy as a whole sinks or soars.

Gender

Like age, gender does not matter. Until recently, entrepreneurship was considered by many to be the last mainstay of male dominance in the business world. This is now recognized as false. Recently, women are increasingly at the helm of new businesses and, with the surge of *work at home* business opportunities, they now have the ability to be entrepreneurial without leaving their home. Many women have started successful companies in recent years—and not just gift shops or snack bars. They are in building contracting, bicycle manufacturing, printing, software, real estate agencies, newspaper publishing, market research, law firms, accounting firms, and more. Although men and women may approach business in a slightly different way, the explosive growth of women-owned businesses over the past decade attests to the success of their non-traditional style.

Marital Status

This is almost irrelevant, but should not be left out. For a woman, being pregnant or having several pre-school children may not provide the best scenario to take the plunge into entrepreneurship. For a man who is the sole support of the family, having two or three children at the university may not be the best time either. But in no way should this discourage them from starting a business. It may mean only that they have to postpone it. Some ideas never happen—only because they come at the wrong time. Ultimately the question is when to start a business, not whether.

Educational Level

We have all heard the phrase *Knowledge is Power!* Knowledge and skills are indeed very important. How they are acquired is less important. Too many college degrees may be a handicap rather than an asset. One researcher suggests that one of the biggest handicaps one can have when starting a business is a Ph.D. For example, Bill Gates, founder of Microsoft, the world's largest software company, quit Harvard after his sophomore year. While the graduate degree may open doors and gives more credibility, a good product or service that satisfies a need is more important.

Cultural Diversity

Is diversity in the air in your office? Are you hiring a workforce that is representative of the consumer base of the business? Several factors are influencing more women and minorities to start their own companies. Most obviously, the percentage of women and minorities in the U.S. workforce is growing, as more women work and immigration increases the population of minorities, so their participation in business ownership is naturally rising as well. For many immigrants, entrepreneurship is the epitome of achieving the American Dream, and therefore business ownership appeals to them.

The Wall Street Journal predicted that as we approached the 21st century, *"managers would have to handle greater cultural diversity"* to be effective. It emphasized that the inability to manage diversity in the workplace would be extremely harmful to the business and cost:

- discrimination lawsuits
- litigation, time, and money
- settlements
- high turnover rates
- negative community image

By understanding what cultural diversity is, why it matters, and how to effectively manage the business in terms of diversity, these risks are minimized.

What is Cultural Diversity?

The idealist will often think of the United States as the great melting pot where anyone, regardless of cultural background, can be assimilated into a single society. However, this ideal vision is not applicable today. A more realistic and appropriate *ideal* is one of multiculturalism or cultural diversity. Multiculturalism is based on the idea that cultural identities should be maintained and valued.

This phenomenon has been, by and large, accepted in American business. Most companies have an increased presence of women and minorities. Diversity has gone from being a legal and ethical negative to a business plus.

Why Does Cultural Diversity Matter?

Cultural diversity is valued by everyone in their professional and personal lives. When a portion of our population is excluded or demoralized, all of us are denied. For businesses and neighborhoods to thrive, we need to be tolerant and sensitive. Our communities are rich with resources. When all segments are respected and utilized, it benefits everyone involved.

Where do we go from here? Can we all strive for change? Can we all be proactive in our decisions and lifestyles rather than reactive to ignorance and intolerance? It is essential to recognize that America is the most diverse nation in the world. Our ethnicity, religion, and life experiences make each of us unique. This means that we all need to learn to accept what is different from us, and respect it.

Managing Cultural Diversity in the Workplace

The management of diversity can be considered a response to the need to recognize, respect and capitalize on the different backgrounds in our society in terms of race, ethnicity, and gender. Different cultural groups have different values, styles, and personalities, each of which may have a substantial effect on the way they do business and all influence the organizational culture or *personality* of the company.

Rather than punishing or stifling these different management styles, employers should recognize these differences as benefits. Diverse management styles can help improve the company's competitive position in the marketplace. If employees resemble the market, that gives the business a competitive edge. When the business works effectively with the community, both the business and the community benefit.

Ethical Issues

For years, ethics and business have been known to have a marriage they are not proud of. One could not ask entrepreneurs to talk about ethics. While stuck in their world, *survival of the fittest* ruled. But it went deeper than that. Entrepreneurs where known as people who defied policies, rules and regulations; and to suggest they should follow a set of pre-established edicts was unheard of.

Entrepreneurs engrossed in starting a business found it a waste of time to think about establishing clear ethical standards for their new companies. They saw ethical issues as the very last item on the *to do* list, if at all.

They felt it was naive to think about being ethical in business; they did not see how it affected the bottom line; or they believed it was something to worry about later, after the company had become successful. While these views were understandable, they were erroneous and perilous.

The term *entrepreneur* was associated with many stereotypical images and phrases. These included a picture of someone selling ice to an Eskimo or a coffin to a dead man. They were also equated with the words *liar*, *cheat* and *dishonest*. When we associated these comments with *entrepreneur*, the word lost credibility and implied there was a clear absence of moral values.

No doubt, one will find many such individuals around today. However, this attitude may be changing. Whether people are hung over from the freewheeling '80s or reflective about this millennium, talk about ethics, values, integrity and responsibility is not only becoming acceptable in the business community, it is now practiced.

If entrepreneurs learn from previous mistakes, they may be more likely to create socially conscious companies—ones that pay higher wages or devote resources to philanthropy. One where flex time is granted to take care of a younger child or an aging parent. They will focus less on maximizing income and more on other goals.

Even those that establish ethical standards are not exempt. The nature of entrepreneurship will fill their life with constant threats arising from limited resources, competition, and the risk of failure. While making business decisions, their actions must concurrently guarantee survival, maximize profit, limit risk, counter the competition, maximize the use of resources, and provide them with internal satisfaction and motivation. Therefore, it is not surprising that priorities will conflict. It is also believed that these entrepreneurial imperatives displace the need to act in morally suitable ways.

Ethical behavior creates an element of trust in business. In an organization with many people who love to cut corners, where products are misrepresented and companies are not forthright about the quality of their goods and services, an established code of ethics can help companies gain credibility and repeat customers.

There is nothing naïve about practicing high ethical standards in business. While there are many unscrupulous organizations, it is erroneous to think that lowering your standards to their level will ensure your company's success, or worse, that their unethical conduct is a justification for your own.

Steps to Establishing an Ethical Policy

Today, many companies have decided to embrace ethics but they have struggled with discovering how to incorporate ethics into their business. Thus, creating and preserving ethics in any organization is an on-going process. And, while it is difficult to anticipate every ethical dilemma that the business will face, or to make the right decision in every situation, it is important to try.

As the business owner, there are many advantages to establishing an ethics policy. You see, ethics come from the top! If the business owner fails to set an example at the top, it is difficult, indeed almost impossible, to persuade the employees that they too should be ethical in their business relationships. A well-defined ethics policy combined with a code of professional conduct provides the foundation for ethical, moral behavior within the company.

In general, an ethics policy should look at the bigger picture of how we connect to society as a whole and what our responsibility is to the greater good. In these days of increasing change and corporate downsizing, some may argue that these principles are idealistic. However, it is important to note that most of those that criticize good ethical practices are focusing on short-term versus long-term results. Organizations that have participated in the downsizing boom are beginning to see how they have traded long-term employee morale and productivity for short-term profit gains.

The bottom line is *what goes around, comes around.* If the business treats the employees with cynicism and lack of respect, chances are the employees will behave in the same way toward the business owner and the customers.

When developing the ethics policy, decide what it is you want the company to stand for, put it in writing, and enforce it. According to Blanchard and Peale, authors of *The Power of Ethical Management*, the ethical policy of the business may be based on five fundamental principles:

Purpose

A purpose combines both the vision and the values that the business owner would like to see upheld in the company. It comes from the top and outlines specifically what is considered acceptable and what is unacceptable in terms of conduct in the business.

Pride

Pride builds dignity and self-respect. If employees are proud of where they work and what they are doing, they are much more apt to act in an ethical manner.

Patience

Since the business owner must focus on long-term versus short-term results, the owner must develop a certain degree of patience. Without it, the owner will become too frustrated and will be more tempted to choose unethical alternatives.

Persistence

Persistence means standing by one's word. It means being committed. If the business owner is not committed to the ethics that have been outlined, then the policy becomes worthless. Stand by your word.

Perspective

In a world where there is never enough time to do everything we need or want to do, it is often difficult to maintain perspective. However, stopping to reflect on where the business is headed, why it is headed that way, and how it is going to get there, allows the business owner to make the best decision both in the short-term as well as the long-term.

Company policy is a reflection of the values deemed important to the business. As the business develops an ethics policy, the focus should be on what the business owner would like the world to be like, not on what others say it resembles. And, as the business owner works to refine the company's ethical standards, remember to walk the talk. Bear in mind that unwritten, unspoken messages can be powerful, too.

6

The Intimidating Stuff!

"I don't have to be the smartest person in the world to succeed. I just need to be smart enough to hire the right people to help me do it."

—David Byrne, founder of BatteriesDirect.com

Legal implications of operating a business

When things are slipping through the cracks or when you feel you are losing control over the growing business, it is time to hire some help and add some brainpower. Depending on the growth goals, the type of person to be hired will vary. If taking it slow, the business owner may just want someone to relieve some of the pressure by performing the routine administrative tasks that are falling behind, such as answering phones, returning calls, opening mail and running errands. Picking up the pace, however, usually involves finding someone who has specialized expertise or who complements the business owner's skills.

Consider the options, and if you feel it is time to hire someone, start with the basics. While you may be tempted to hire the first person who displays interest, doing that can cause a small company too much money. As an entrepreneur, you cannot afford to just have a body. You need to have the right candidate for the position. Start by evaluating the job that needs to be accomplished. Write down the skills that are necessary, the duties that will be assigned, and the characteristics you will be looking for in the person you would like to hire. Write the job description. Outline the specifics of what needs to be done, the reporting structure, experience or knowledge necessary.

As the business grows and more employees are hired, the scope of responsibility increases as more regulations and laws come into play, but having even one employee requires knowledge and diligence in seeking the answers to the compliance questions. Business owners often do not have the time to search out the appropriate agency and regulations, or to complete the necessary paperwork.

Employment regulations are complicated. There are state and federal requirements governing aspects of every business and there are other regulations specific to each industry and profession. Many states have a clearing-house for employment-related information.

The following is a brief synopsis of some of the federal statutes governing employers, which may apply to your business. Obviously, the statutes themselves are much more detailed. This list is a representative sampling of the potentially applicable statutes. Whether or not these laws apply to the business may be determined by the **number of employees** working for it, so if the business is growing, be sure you are aware of the rules that apply accordingly. As the owner, consult with a lawyer to gain an awareness of the laws that are applicable to your business. Many states have additional or more restrictive laws governing employment. Generally, when state and federal laws conflict, the law that is most favorable to the employee and more restrictive to the employer must be followed.

FAIR LABOR STANDARDS ACT:

- Addresses minimum wage and overtime
- Establishes a standard 40-hour work week and requires time and a half payment for hours worked in excess of 40 per week for non-exempt employees
- Exempts certain classifications of employees from overtime pay requirements
- Sets minimum age for employment
- Sets minimum hourly wage rate and minimum wage for most workers
- Applies to employers involved in interstate commerce with two or more employees
- Does the company's personnel policy address work hours and overtime?

SOCIAL SECURITY:

- Establishes a number of social programs which have the basic objectives of providing for the material needs of individuals and families

- Programs include: retirement insurance; survivor's insurance; disability insurance; hospital and medical insurance for the aged, disabled; and supplemental security income, among others

- Reports of earnings must be filed annually by every employer who is required to withhold income tax from wages and/or who is liable for FICA taxes, also called Social Security and Medicare taxes

- Each employer must:

  A. Keep a record of the name and Social Security number of each employee as it is shown on the employee's Social Security card (this information will be needed for the earnings report); and

  B. Get an employer identification number from IRS by filing an application (Form SS-4) which may be obtained from any IRS or Social Security office (this number must be shown on the employer's tax returns and earnings reports)

- The **Social Security Handbook** is available online at http://www.ssa.gov

MEDICARE, FICA:

- Medicare is the U.S.'s health insurance program

- FICA stands for Federal Insurance Contributions Act

- The Federal Insurance Contributions Act (FICA) tax includes two separate taxes: one is the Social Security tax and the other is the Medicare tax

- Different **tax rates** apply for each, and generally the rates change each year

- Taxes are paid by both employer and employee (withheld from wages)

EQUAL PAY ACT:

- Prohibits discrimination in pay on the basis of sex where jobs are performed under similar conditions and require equal skill, effort and responsibility

- Permits pay differentials between sexes where such differences are based on seniority systems, merit systems, wage incentive plans, or factors other than sex

IMMIGRATION REFORM and CONTROL ACT:

- Requires employers to verify that applicants for employment are authorized to work in the United States
- Civil and criminal penalties for knowingly employing unauthorized aliens
- Prohibits discrimination based on national origin or citizenship if the alien is authorized to work
- Enforced by the Department of Justice and the Immigration and Naturalization Service

FEDERAL UNEMPLOYMENT TAX ACT:

- Provides workers' payments for a given period of time or until they find a new job, if job was terminated through no fault of their own
- Unemployment insurance is based on federal and state systems, with employers receiving a credit against the federal tax for state taxes paid
- Which employees are eligible for compensation, the amount they receive, and the period of time benefits are paid, are determined by a mix of federal and state law

OSHA ACT OF 1970:

US Dept. of Labor—Occupational Safety & Health Administration

- OSHA requires all employers to provide a workplace that is free from recognized hazards that cause, or are likely to cause, death or serious physical harm to employees
- Establishes the Occupational Safety and Health Administration, which is responsible for workplace safety standards and regulations for various industries.

TITLE VII CIVIL RIGHTS ACT:

- Prohibits discrimination in hiring, firing, promoting, compensation, or terms, conditions, or privileges of employment on the basis of race, color, sex, religion, or national origin
- Permits discrimination in employment on the basis of race, religion, sex, or national origin where any of these factors are bona fide occupational qualifications necessary to the operation of the enterprise

- Permits bona fide seniority, merit, or incentive systems that have the effect of discriminating provided such systems are not the result of an intention to discriminate
- Applies to employers with 15 or more employees, employment agencies, unions, state and local governments
- Enforced by the Equal Employment Opportunity Commission

AMERICANS WITH DISABILITIES ACT:

- Prohibits discrimination in employment on the basis of physical or mental impairments that limit one or more major life activities. These impairments may be real or perceived
- Requires that reasonable accommodation be made for handicapped individuals

PREGNANCY DISCRIMINATION ACT:

- Prohibits discrimination in employment based on pregnancy, childbirth, or related medical condition
- Applies to employers with 15 or more employees, unions with 25 members, employment agencies, federal, state and local governments

AGE DISCRIMINATION IN EMPLOYMENT ACT (ADEA):

- Prohibits discrimination against individuals over 40 with respect to hiring, compensation, terms, conditions and privileges of employment on the basis of age
- Eliminates mandatory retirement age for employees (with some exceptions, e.g. pilots)
- Applies to employers with 20 employees; unions with 25 members; employment agencies, federal, state and local governments
- Enforced by the Equal Employment Opportunity Commission

OLDER WORKER BENEFIT PROTECTION ACT:

- Amendment to the Age Discrimination in Employment Act
- Prohibits discrimination with respect to employee benefits on the basis of age

- It also regulates early retirement incentive programs
- Enforced by the Equal Employment Opportunity Commission

COBRA:

- Found in the "Consolidated Omnibus Budget Reconciliation Act", hence the name "COBRA"
- Pertains to continuing group health insurance when employment is terminated
- Requires employer to continue to include ex-employees in employer's group health plan. Full cost of health insurance must be paid by employee
- Information about COBRA rights must be provided to employee on the date of separation
- Administered by the U. S. Department of Labor—Pension and Welfare Benefits Administration

FAMILY MEDICAL LEAVE ACT (FMLA):

- FMLA requires that employers provide up to 12 weeks of unpaid leave, within any 12 month period, to employees for the care of a newborn or adopted child, for the care of a seriously ill family member, or for treatment and care of the employee's own serious medical condition
- Applies to employers with 50 or more employees
- Enforced by the Wage and Hour Division of the Department of Labor

WARN ACT:

- Worker Adjustment and Retraining Notification Act
- Requires that employers give 60 days advance notice to employees of impending plant closings or layoffs involving 50 or more employees
- Applies to employers with 100 or more employees

ERISA:

- Employee Retirement Income Security Act
- Governs the operation of pensions and retirement benefits provided by employers to their employees

- Does not require that employers provide such benefits, but regulates the conduct of employers that do provide such plans

- Enforced by the Pension and Welfare Benefits Administration of the Department of Labor

The Hiring Process

Hiring employees can be a very time-consuming process. Before starting the search, consider how one of the current employees may be able to successfully fill a vacant position. In this case, the business owner is already familiar with the employee's capabilities, work habits, productivity, and contributions to the business. Promoting internal candidates is also a good opportunity to demonstrate the opportunities for advancement in the company.

When searching for job candidates, do not limit the search to just one approach. Use various avenues so that the company attracts the right candidates, and make sure the cost and value are in line with the company's recruiting goals.

Temporary Employment Agencies

These agencies can provide a wide range of employees with various professional or administrative skill sets. Temporary employees are hired on a short-term basis. However, based on their performance the business owner may decide to offer a permanent position. Check to see how much the temporary employment agency will charge if the business does decide to hire one of their temporary workers full-time.

Headhunters

Many companies rely on executive search firms, or headhunters, to locate good candidates for important positions. The two types of executive recruiters include:

1. Contingency Firms—generally appropriate for entry-level or mid-level management positions with clearly defined requirements. They are paid when they fill a position.

2. Retained Firms—a good choice for top-level general management and board-of-directors recruiting. They are paid regardless of the outcome of a particular search.

A standard practice in the executive search industry is to charge a percentage of the new executive's first-year compensation. For contingency firms, the usual range is 20 to 25 percent or higher. For retained firms, the usual range is 33 to 35 percent.

Contract Recruiters

These recruiters are paid to act as consultants to the company, and can hire every type of employee the company needs. Any time a company is trying to hire more than a handful of people at once, a contract recruiter can lead the process of sourcing, scheduling, screening resumés, and communicating with candidates.

Company Website

Advertising job positions on the company website is a good and cost-efficient way to publicize upcoming job opportunities and allow the user to obtain information on the company. Having a company website that provides a wealth of information will ensure that anyone who applies for a job listed there will be aware of the company's vision, services and operations.

Want Ads

Placing want ads in local and regional newspapers, trade magazines, and weekly publications offers a typical means of announcing job opportunities to a wide audience of potential employees. Writing a strong want ad gives a better idea of who the business is looking for and offers potential candidates a better idea of whether the position is right for them. Be as specific as possible about the needs and the precise level of the open position (i.e. job title, position description, and salary range), and make sure to include the minimum requirements of the job (i.e. education, experience, and skills).

The Internet

Millions of job seekers surf the Web each day, post their resumés, fill out online applications, and even conduct online or telephone interviews. The Internet makes huge numbers of candidates available to any firm with access to the Web. Read the fine print. Be aware that significant fees may be required to join.

Industry Journals and Professional Associations

If the business is looking to fill specialized positions, the owner may want to post job listings in member communications. This is an inexpensive way to connect directly with people who understand the industry.

Area Technical Schools, Universities or Colleges

Many schools provide job listings in the form of a newsletter or an online job database. Choosing the right schools can help the owner zero in on a dedicated pool of high-potential candidates. Contact the Career Centers and ask for the posting requirements. Often these ads are free and provide the opportunity to hire interns who will work for free in exchange for the experience or academic credit.

Employee Referral Rewards

Inform employees about job openings at the business and encourage them to refer good candidates; offer cash bonuses or rewards to employees who success-fully recruit someone to work for the company, as long as the recruit stays longer than three months. These rewards can range from a few hundred to a thousand dollars, depending on how difficult it is to find employees to fill the position.

Word-of-Mouth

Often the best prospective employees are the people referred by trusted friends and associates. Get the word out about the business and demonstrate to the can-didates how a job there fits with their career goals. Go to trade shows, community activities, local association meetings, and other events where the business owner can meet potential employees and promote the company. Outline the company's vision; highlight the team spirit; speak candidly about the firm's challenges; and present information about the business clearly and in an exciting way.

Screening the Candidates

Once the bulk of responses are received, narrow the stack of resumés to the top 10 candidates and start by preparing a basic list of interview questions. As the owner, consider a brief telephone interview with the top applicants before sched-uling their face-to-face interviews. Some candidates may look good on paper, but will make a terrible telephone impression. When calling an applicant in for an interview, qualities to look for include good communication skills, a neat and professional appearance, and a friendly and enthusiastic manner. Remember to take objective notes during the interview to help compare candidates when it is time to make a final decision. Following are some tips to help you to screen can-didates and improve your job interviewing skills.

Set the framework of the interview

Discuss the interview format with the applicant, provide an introduction and put the candidate at ease by outlining the basic structure of the interview. Have the applicant feel comfortable to speak freely and provide detailed answers to the questions. Be prepared to discuss the business's core functions, history, plans, and culture. As the owner, prepare a fact sheet that lists relevant company information.

Avoid questions with an obvious response

Try to avoid general questions. Avoid any question that can be answered with a simple YES or NO. The idea is to find out how the person will perform in a specific role. Formulate the questions based on the list of desired skills.

Encourage candidates to talk about themselves

To avoid pre-planned responses, construct open-ended questions that invite candidates to share information and talk about their experiences in detail. Have a good mix of experienced-based, work-style-based, and behavior-based questions that will provide a complete view of the candidate's background and personality. These questions will help gather some real information about the applicant's judgment, willingness to take risks, decision-making capabilities and ability to work in a team environment. Following are some examples:

Experienced-based

1. What were your three biggest accomplishments in your last job? In your career?

2. Tell me about a recent project you have completed.

3. When working on a group project, what role do you typically play? Why?

4. Tell me about a time you had to make a critical decision, and what went into that process.

5. What are three things you really do well?

6. What are three areas where you need help?

Work-style-based

1. Describe a typical day on your current job.

2. What do you like (about your job)?

3. What don't you like?

4. How would you react in a scenario that would require you to work independently?

5. In what situations have you disagreed with your boss?

6. What was the outcome?

7. What risks did you take in your last job and what were the results?

8. What methods do you use to make decisions?

Behavior-based

1. Describe three situations where your work was criticized.

2. Tell me about the last time that you missed a project deadline. What happened, and how did you manage the problem?

3. What is the best environment for you to function in?

4. What would your best reference, or people you work with, say about you?

5. What *wouldn't* they say?

Questions not to ask during an interview

The law is very strict about what you *cannot* ask during an interview, and asking them can lead to a discrimination lawsuit. Questions on non-job related information such as age, race, marital status or disability are legally forbidden. When conducting an interview it is advisable to stick to professional topics.

Sample questions of what not to ask include:

1. How old are you?

2. Are you married?

3. Are you a citizen?

4. Are you planning to have children soon?

5. Are you disabled?

6. Do you have any medical problems?

7. Have you ever filed for worker's compensation?

Bringing the interview to a close

1. Leave time at the end of the interview for the applicant to ask questions, and pay attention to what he/she asks.

2. Based on the kind of questions asked you will be able to judge if the applicant has researched your company, or is only interested in what can be got out of the job.

3. End the interview by letting the candidate know what to expect next and when to expect to hear from you.

4. Take five or 10 minutes to write down the applicant's outstanding qualities and evaluate his or her personality and skills against your job description and specifications.

Keeping up with the Paperwork!

New employers need to be aware of the various requirements for hiring employees. Specifically, it is important to know: what you must do if you have employees, how you must satisfy wage-reporting requirements, and EIN (Employer Identification Numbers). Hiring employees also creates new responsibilities between you and federal and state government agencies.

When hiring employees, new forms are required to be filled out. These include the I-9, the W-4, and the W-5 (if the employee qualifies for advance payments of the earned income credit).

Form I–9

Allows the business owner to verify that each new employee is legally eligible to work in the United States. Both the owner and the employee must complete the Immigration and Naturalization Service (INS) Form I–9, Employment Eligibility Verification. The form may be obtained from INS offices or from the INS web site at www.ins.usdoj.gov. Call the INS at (800) 375-5283 for more information about your responsibilities.

Form W–4

Each employee must fill out Form W–4, Employee's Withholding Allowance Certificate. The business will use the filing status and withholding allowances shown on this form to figure the amount of income tax to withhold from the employee's wages. Each year, remind the employees to submit a new Form W-4 if they need to change their withholding. For detailed instructions for completing Form W-4 see Publication 505, Tax Withholding and Estimating Tax.

Form W–5

An eligible employee who has a qualifying child is entitled to receive advance earned income credit (EIC) payments with his or her pay during the year. To get these payments, the employee must provide a completed Form W–5, Earned Income Credit Advance Payment Certificate. The business owner is required to make advance EIC payments to employees who turn in a completed and signed Form W–5. For more information see Publication 15.

Name and Social Security Number

Record each new employee's name and social security number from his or her social security card. Any employee without a social security card should apply for one. The Social Security Administration (SSA) offers social security number (SSN) verification and quick access to relevant forms and publications.

Employment Taxes

Employers are generally required to withhold employment taxes from their employees' wages and manage federal, state, and local taxes. Federal employment taxes include: Federal income tax withholding, Social Security and Medicare taxes, and Federal Unemployment (FUTA) taxes. For further information about your federal requirements with regard to employees, you will need to obtain Publication 15, Circular E, Employer's Tax Guide.

7

Help Wanted!

○ ○

"I studied the lives of great men and famous women, and I found that the men and women who got to the top were those who did the jobs they had in hand, with everything they had of energy and enthusiasm and hard work."

—Harry Truman, US President

Building Beyond One

Once everything is in place, how does one grow the business? The key to success is creative marketing and excellent customer service. Experiment with ways to reach potential customers. Then, keep them coming back by exceeding their expectations. If everything was done right, the business will now be thriving, you find yourself working long hours and are having trouble following up with customers in a timely manner. The finances have been evaluated and the projected growth has been calculated, and it is time for the business to expand. You have hired an extra pair of hands. How do you train the employee? What resources are provided? How do you get him or her to buy into the vision and help you achieve the business goals? The best route is to create a handbook that will serve as the roadmap.

Human Resources Handbook

Starting up a business can be great fun but it is also hard work. One of the most important aspects of running a business is having a talented group of employees. Finding those good employees is crucial to most businesses. The better the employees, the more likely the company will be successful. However, a few things need to be taken care of before hiring the first employee.

The first step is to become informed about employment laws regulated by the state where the business is located. Payroll regulation is the most important, and any local accountant can help ensure the business meets payroll compliance. If that is not possible then consider outsourcing the payroll to a payroll service provider.

As the owner, familiarize yourself with the Fair Labor Standards Act (FLSA) for wage and hour laws; the Immigration Reform and Control Act (IRCA) in order to comply with having an I-9 for each of the employees. The Fair Labor Standards Act (FLSA) is a federal law enforced by the Employment Standards Administration (ESA). It mandates labor standards such as breaks, overtime and minimum wages for employees. Many states have additional requirements. Check the state's wage and hour laws for more information.

The Occupational Safety and Health Act (OSHA) oversees safety in the workplace. However, states have their own safety laws sometimes called *baby OSHA*. Check the states requirements and regulations. Does the business need workers' compensation insurance? YES, even if the business only has one employee. Once you learn and become aware of all the rules and regulations, make sure the business is ready to hire staff.

There are many good ways to find talented individuals to work for the company.

Temporary agencies provide businesses with a variety of workers: accountants, programmers, sales personnel, secretaries and much more. One good thing about temporary employees is businesses get the opportunity to see how the workers perform, with the possibility to roll them over to a permanent position. Keep in mind that temp agencies sometimes charge a fee if the business does not hire the temps on a full-time basis. When hiring a temp agency read the fine print in the contract before signing on the dotted line.

Much like a Temporary Agency, Employment agencies provide workers, but mostly only permanent employees, for a fee. They usually have a long list of resumés and have done a screening and reference check of the workers. The business should be cautious of these firms as well for the same reasons. Again, read the fine print!

Traditional ways of finding employees are few and far between because of the high use of Internet technology. One way of searching for employees is to post a job vacancy announcement on the company website. If the company does not have a website use job websites such as Monster, Careerbuilder, and HotJobs.

These offer affordable prices and allow the business to reach millions of people, who are already using the system.

Finding those talented employees is a bit complicated, and if the business owner does not have the right interviewing skills, the business will risk losing a good candidate. In a competitive job market, conducting effective interviews is essential. There are many questions that should *not* be asked during a job interview, because they could make the business vulnerable to a charge of discrimination if the prospective employee is not hired. Businesses also have to be careful about information volunteered by potential employees for the same reasons. Take comfort in the fact that most *illegal* questions are unrelated to any legitimate hiring criteria.

Here are the general types of questions to avoid: How old are you? Any other age-related questions; What is your religious background?; Do you have a disability?; Are you planning to have children?; Are you married?; What is your maiden name?; Are you an American citizen? Rather than focusing on what you should not say, focus on things that are relevant, such as education, job skills and job history. By staying away from forbidden areas and remaining professional, the interviews should be fine.

Now that the business has taken the first step to staffing, what do you do? Well you narrowed down the search to a few candidates and need to pay them if they get hired right? What do you do now? Any small business owner can tell you that paying employees involves a lot more than writing a check every two weeks. There are dozens of laws governing employee compensation. The business has to be well organized and stay up to date on federal and state guidelines. The key to staying on top of things is setting up a system that complies with all the applicable state and federal laws.

Payroll

To get started, try this step-by-step approach to setting up a simple payroll system:

Step 1: Get an Employer Identification Number (EIN). IRS Form SS-4.

Step 2: Get state and local identification numbers if they are required in the area or areas where your business operates.

Step 3: Separate the independent contractors and full-time employees. The business does not have to withhold taxes from an independent contractor's pay.

However, classifying all of the employees as independent contractors could heavily penalize the business. For more information visit the IRS website and read the IRS Publication 15 Circular E, The Employer's Tax Guide.

Step 4: Have each employee fill out and sign IRS Form W-4. New workers should fill out a W-4 as soon as possible. The form must be filled out every time there is a qualifying event such as marriage or divorce, birth of children, gain or loss of a dependent, or change of withholding amounts for any other reasons. If the business does not have an employee's W-4 on file, the business is required by law to treat the employee, for withholding purposes, as a single person with no exemptions.

Step 5: Establish a pay period. Most states require that employers pay workers on regular paydays. Check with the state department of labor for the state's specific guidelines.

Step 6: Establish payroll records. For federal tax purposes, keep the following information on file:

- The name, address and Social Security Number of each employee
- The total amount and date of each payment
- The portion of each payment that constituted taxable wages
- Copies of each employee's W-4
- Dates and amounts of tax deposits
- Copies of returns you filed
- Copies of any undeliverable W-2 forms.

Step 7: Decide if the business will pay workers for time spent in orientation, sick days, meals or working from home. Your state department of labor can tell you if you are required to pay for this time.

Step 8: Check local overtime rules. According to most state laws, any work that exceeds 40 hours per week must be compensated with at least one and a half times the employee's hourly wage.

Step 9: Figure out what needs to be withheld. The IRS expects a business to withhold a portion of every employee's paycheck. Chances are your state and even local governments require withholding as well. The government provides tax tables that calculate the amount that must be withheld once the business has established the appropriate amount of taxable wages. All states except Alaska, Florida, Nevada, New Hampshire, South Dakota, Tennessee, Texas, Washington and Wyoming impose a personal income tax. Like the federal government, most states provide tables to help the business compute withholding amounts.

As addressed before, many business owners save time and reduce the risk of errors by hiring a bookkeeper or payroll service. An outside payroll person or service can perform basic payroll-related tasks, deposit tax payments, prepare W-2s and take care of insurance and retirement plans.

Because payroll is so complicated, many businesses use an outside service. The cost of using one of these services averages about $3 per check. Some service providers are ADP and PayChex. In general, outsourcing payroll can cost half of what it would to do it in-house. Hiring an outside service also eliminates the need to hire a full-time payroll manager, and the business owner can free up time to work on other aspects of the business.

If outsourcing payroll is a choice, make sure to get at least three quotes before deciding on a payroll service. Many payroll firms facilitate this right on their websites. Speak with other small business owners who outsource their payroll to find out how much they pay and if they are satisfied with their service.

Employee Handbook

The next step in the process is to begin to think about an employee handbook, when hiring someone as an employee, establish a working relationship with him or her. Setting the parameters of that relationship as quickly as possible will minimize the potential for future conflicts. An employee handbook is an excellent way to define those parameters. It sets down your policies in black and white where any worker can find them and helps ensure that employees are treated fairly and equally.

To avoid any legal problems, make sure these six essential elements are included in your company's handbook:

The disclaimer

Every employee manual should have a disclaimer that states expressly that the handbook is not a contract of employment. Without such a notice, a fired employee might attempt to sue for breach of contract. It is a good idea to include that phrase on the Cover and on the Acknowledgment of Receipt page.

Employee definitions

Distinguish between full-time staff and contract employees, but avoid using the word *permanent*. *Permanent full-time* and *permanent part-time* are not good definitions from a legal standpoint. Calling workers permanent implies an arrangement that cannot be terminated under any circumstances, an implication that could make it difficult to fire an unsatisfactory worker.

Sexual harassment policy

Make it clear that sexual harassment or any such conduct will not be tolerated in the business. Always designate more than one person with whom an employee can file a complaint.

Work week

Define the work week as the seven-day period within which overtime is calculated. Never specify a *normal* work week of Monday through Friday. Otherwise, employees might refuse to work after five o'clock during the week or at all during the weekend.

Vacation policy

Specify that vacations must be approved. That way the business can still be flexible, but it will be able to maintain adequate staffing throughout the year.

Acknowledgement of Receipt

At the very end of the employee handbook, make sure to include an acknowledgement of receipt page that states the disclaimer as well as the understanding of the policies. Make sure to include a phrase that states the information contained in the employee handbook is subject to change. The sheet must have a space for the employee to sign and it needs to be turned in and placed in the employee's file.

For organizational and legal purposes, maintain and update an employment file on each employee. The employee file must contain the following: resumé, references, employment application, original job description, performance evaluation, W-4 and I-9 among other things. Be sure to make a copy of all forms that an employee signs. By law, employees are entitled to a copy of anything that they sign, and they can request to see anything in their employee file.

Having an employee handbook, a payroll system and employees, the entrepreneur is well on the way to managing the business, but that is not all that needs to be managed. An entrepreneur also has to manage the employees. Always remember to treat the employees as you yourself would like to be treated. Entrepreneurs need to foster a working relationship with those they hire in order to develop and promote trust and loyalty. Not many business owners receive any kind of formal management training.

Here are some of the key things to do to keep employees happy, motivated and loyal.

Communicate the big picture

If you want the employees to work hard and be loyal, keep them informed. Open communication helps foster loyalty and gives employees a sense of importance and pride. It helps them understand how their work contributes to the company's success.

Delegate work and responsibilities

Share the workload with the employees. Delegate projects according to people's strengths and weaknesses, and let employees develop their own good work habits and leadership skills.

Help employees prioritize

Setting deadlines and goals helps keep employees focused and busy, and motivates them to do their work. Talk to each employee about the company's goals, and work with them to set individual goals directly linked to the mission of the business.

Recognize problems

Be pro-active and resolve situations before they get out of hand. If you notice a change in an employee's work habits or attitude, try to get to the root of the problem before it starts affecting the rest of the staff.

Reward employees

Recognize a worker's contribution, by simply saying *thank you*. Whether you do it with words, money, an employee-of-the-month program or other incentives, make sure employees know you value their efforts and contributions. But always keep in mind what motivates each employee, and personalize the reward. Everybody appreciates raises and bonuses, but monetary rewards are not the only way to thank employees for a job well done.

Give reviews

Employees need feedback about their performance, to improve their skills and grow professionally. Set up a formal review program and give performance appraisals once or twice a year.

Be humane

Show employees some compassion by being flexible with work hours and time off so they can tend to important matters. Employees always appreciate a considerate boss. As long as the business does not suffer, make every effort to accommodate workers who have special needs.

Take the time to be a manager

During busy times, when work is piling up, do not forget to be a manager. Employees depend on their boss's strength and guidance, especially when they are stressed out or faced with new projects that require your time and input. Give employees your undivided attention when they want to talk.

Be a leader

Walk the talk. Lead by example. Leadership is ACTION; not position!

Warren Bennis, popular writer on leadership, and business professor at the University of Southern California, shares this view. "There is a profound difference between management and leadership, and both are important. To manage means to bring about, to accomplish, to have charge of or responsibility for, to conduct. Leading is influencing, guiding in a direction, course, action, and opinion. The distinction is crucial". One of Bennis's most quoted phrases is, "Managers are people who do things right and leaders are people who do the right thing." Bennis further defines the difference using the following paired contrasts.

- The manager administers; the leader innovates
- The manager maintains; the leader develops.
- The manager accepts reality; the leader investigates it.

- The manager focuses on systems and structures; the leader focuses on people.
- The manager relies on control; the leader inspires trust.
- The manager has a short-range view; the leader has a long-range perspective.
- The manager asks how and when; the leader asks what and why.
- The manager has his or her eye always on the bottom line; the leader has his or her eye on the horizon.
- The manager imitates; the leader originates.
- The manager accepts the status quo; the leader challenges it.
- The manager is the classic good soldier; the leader is his or her own person.

Just as there are items to include in an employee handbook, there are also things you should omit. You must pay special attention to sensitive legal topics and avoid documenting policies in the following areas.

Overtime restrictions

Never require that overtime work be authorized in advance.

Regulations limiting workers' rights as parents or potential parents

Never require that an employee disclose facts or plans related to pregnancy. Adhere to laws that regulate maternity or family leave and related issues.

Anti-romance rules

Such bans are difficult to enforce and infringe upon workers' personal freedom.

Rules about giving notice

Never require that an employee give notice before quitting.

Rules requiring workers to keep information about their compensation to themselves

Labor laws protect an employee's right to discuss such work-related issues with other employees.

Employee Benefits

The only legally required benefit employers are obligated to maintain is workers' compensation insurance; or be self-insured. There is no such requirement for independent contractors. However, to protect against potential exposure for work-related accidents involving contractors and other third parties, a business should maintain liability insurance.

Employee benefits become a matter of marketplace competition, part of a total compensation package to attract and retain employees. The variety and generosity of benefits typically depends on the size of the business, its resources and bargaining power in the benefits arena.

If you are looking to offer health benefits, there are a few options. Two health insurance options are usually sufficient for most start-up organizations. Give employees a choice between a health maintenance organization (HMO) and a preferred provider organization (PPO).

Although HMO and PPO monthly premiums are roughly the same, each plan has fundamental differences that can influence an employee's choice. HMOs have lower out-of-pocket costs and no deductibles as long as the insured uses providers in the HMO network. PPOs have deductibles but offer more flexibility than HMOs, allowing the insured to choose from a wider selection of doctors and specialists outside of the PPO network.

Allowing employees to choose between an HMO and a PPO gives them the freedom to pick the plan that best suits their needs. It also shows them that their employer cares enough about their individual situations to provide them with two different health insurance options.

Good benefits are a key component of employee satisfaction and retention. Let us focus on vacation and sick leave. Traditionally, companies have set up programs where employees get a certain number of days for paid sick leave and a certain number of days for paid vacation. This type of plan is easy to institute. Simply decide how many sick days and vacation days to give employees per year (put this information in the employee handbook).

While this system works well for many companies, consider altering it to give employees more respect and autonomy. There are ways to do it so as not to incur additional costs. For example, some companies pool these different types of leave into a unified bank of hours that employees can draw on. Instead of giving employees 10 vacation days and 5 sick days a year, give each person 120 hours of paid time off a year to use as they see fit.

This plan has many benefits. First, it allows employees to schedule days off without having to tell any white lies. It also means that employees do not feel cheated when they are not eligible for certain types of leave. What good does it do to give employees time off to be with sick kids if an employee has no children? The great thing about this plan is that employees get choices for using their time off. They may use it for vacation, personal time or sick days, or they can just accumulate it. It's like a savings account. Some employers even allow employees who accrue more than a predetermined amount of paid time off—80 hours for example—to redeem the excess hours by exchanging them for cash at the worker's current pay scale.

The amount of paid leave or time off given to employees is up to the business owner, but there are industry standards to keep in mind. On average, new employees usually get about 17 or 18 days off per year, allocated evenly between sick and vacation days. Professional, long-term employees could accrue 30 or more days off a year. To learn more about the norms in the industry, check the Chamber of Commerce salary and benefits reports for the state the business operates in.

When starting out, there seem to be many things to think about, but think of it as a wheel. Once it gets rolling there is no stopping it.

Outsourcing

Outsourcing has been mentioned previously. However, in this section we will define outsourcing and list several functions and issues to think about related to choosing whether to outsource or not.

According to Michelle Dunn, owner of MAD Collection Agency, outsourcing is when an organization uses outside, independent workers to execute tasks. In essence outsourcing is paying someone to do a business function that would otherwise cost too much or take up too much of your time. One thing to keep in mind is that there is a difference between sourcing and outsourcing. *Sourcing* is all about determining *who* will do *what* to fulfill enterprise responsibilities. Outsourcing is all about using sources that are external to the enterprise.

Typically, there are two types of outsourced services: technology and business process. They each can be broken into the following areas. Technology Services: Electronic Commerce; Network Infrastructure; Software; Telecommunications; and Website Development & Hosting. Business Process Outsourcing: Customer Relations Management; Equipment; Finance; Accounting; Human Resources; Logistics; Procurement; Supply Chain Management; and Security.

As a business owner who is outsourcing, or thinking about outsourcing, it is imperative to understand what it means to have an outsourcing strategy. Here are some things to ponder: why you are outsourcing and what are you outsourcing? How do internal and external sources interrelate? Are they interdependent? What is the value expected from the outsourcing deals? and finally, how is that value translated to requirements, service levels and prices?

Many reasons can lead a business to outsource. They include:

- The business is not keeping pace with changes in technology
- High inventory costs or high personnel turnover
- Information technology budget is not affordable
- Poor internal and/or external customer service
- Lower costs due to economies of scale
- Ability to concentrate on core functions
- Greater flexibility and ability to define the requisite service more readily
- Less dependency upon internal resources
- Control of budget
- Faster set-up of the function or service
- Lower ongoing investment required in internal infrastructure
- Lack of internal expertise
- Increase flexibility to meet changing business conditions
- Purchase of industry best practice
- Improve risk management
- Acquire innovative ideas
- Increase commitment and energy in non-core areas
- Improve credibility and image by associating with superior providers
- Generate cash by transferring assets to the provider
- Gain market access and business opportunities through the supplier's network
- Turn fixed costs into variable costs

Despite the size of this list, every scenario is different. There may well be equally compelling arguments against any sort of outsourcing arrangement. As a business owner, take full advantage of the benefits outsourcing has to offer. Getting it right is a challenge and common pitfalls should be avoided. If outsourcing is an option because it will remove a headache, help the business with its strategy, or poorly managed operations, outsourcing can be tragic.

Pursuing an outsourcing strategy to "remove a headache"

Operational headaches can be cured, and outsourcing is indeed one of the ways of doing so, but that should not be the primary motivation.

Treating outsourcing as a monolithic, oversimplified strategic concept

This can prevent managers from exploring other, potentially more beneficial options. Outsourcing is related to, but is not the same as, moving operations offshore, relocating operations or functions within a geographic area, and sharing and centralizing services. In addition to the various *hows* of outsourcing, there are many other questions. Do we outsource an entire function, or just selected services? Do we enter into a long-term agreement, or conduct a series of short-term *experiments*? Do we multi-source to several vendors at once, or find a single outsourcing partner?

Outsourcing poorly managed operations in the hopes that someone else can manage them better

This is a way of trading one headache for another. While it is critical for value chain partners in an outsourcing relationship to play to their relative strengths, outsourcing something that the business does not know how to manage or understand can lead to problems later on. How can the business set the standard if it does not understand what is going on?

Overcoming the problems of poorly managed operations, finding and following a sound approach to outsourcing, and monitoring market developments, are all very much about implementation and execution. Outsourcing is not something to be taken lightly. It can make or break the business.

8

What Flavor is Your Lemonade?

Diversity Issues in Entrepreneurship

Despite great progress, minority businesses have a long way to go. Blacks, Hispanics, Asians and other minorities make up 27 percent of the U.S. population, but own only 14.5 percent of the nation's companies and take in 3 percent of all business revenue. Minorities, including women and the disabled, have to work harder to succeed as entrepreneurs.

The Minority Entrepreneur

Entrepreneurship is booming among America minority groups. According to the latest U.S. Census Bureau data, the number of African American-owned firms grew by more than 26 percent and Hispanic firms grew by 30 percent. (Meanwhile, total U.S. business grew by only 6 percent.) Essential to that growth has been the availability of federal programs, information and resources for minorities—including mentoring.

If you're a minority entrepreneur, your chances of successfully starting and growing your small business are greatly increased when a business mentor (and advice) play a role in your business's development. Contact SCORE to learn how you can benefit from small business counseling and mentoring programs, as well as seminars and workshops geared toward helping entrepreneurs start and run their businesses.

Women Entrepreneurs

According to the Small Business Administration, women business owners are critically important to the American economy. America's 9.1 million women-owned businesses employ 27.5 million people and contribute $3.6 trillion to the economy. However, women continue to face unique obstacles in the world of business although they are starting businesses at twice the rate of their male counterparts.

Women entrepreneurs are transforming the economy at a speed that startles those who have analyzed the demographic composition of American business. Throughout the Nation, women-owned businesses have grown steadily during the last ten years.

According to the Women's Business Institute (April 1997), women have become a major force in the economy. While employment by large corporations is generally decreasing, employment by women-owned businesses is growing. In fact, women-owned businesses now are employing 35 percent more people in the U.S. than the companies in the Fortune 500 are employing worldwide.

Women business owners have worked hard to get where they are. They typically do not inherit family businesses. They tend to start their own businesses to satisfy a personal need or to overcome the lack of advancement in the traditional job market. They often start businesses to solve problems faced by women, problems that the marketplace has failed to address, especially in areas of family well-being, childcare, healthcare, education, and fashion.

Women-owned businesses have a different culture. They are generally smaller, faster and more efficient. Studies show that it is more likely for them to offer flex-time, tuition reimbursement, and telecommuting, than U.S. businesses generally offer. The reason for this is that women are finding solutions to problems that have traditionally held them back in the workplace.

Men versus Women Entrepreneurs

According to the Ohio Women's Business Resource Network (Columbus, OH April 1997), these are the main differences between Men and Women Entrepreneurs:

- Many women business owners view business ownership with different concerns and interests than their male counterparts. Although some women business owners are interested in a large, profitable organization, many prefer their new business to be small, friendly and easy to manage.

Because growth usually equals structure, many women business owners choose to remain small to avoid dealing with an organization that would require layers of management and a culture that might lack support or is rigid, unfriendly, or limiting.

- Women start their businesses for a variety of reasons. Independence, flexibility, freedom from corporate limitations, and the freedom to take risks are usually major motivational factors for the woman who decides to start her own business. In addition, many women seek personal satisfaction, a certain balance, broader horizons, the respect of the industry, the excitement of growth, and the opportunity to learn new things.

- Women start their organizations to create a secure future and to have choices about their lifestyles. Many have a community mission that they plan to support or fund. Many want to provide good jobs and a secure future for a dedicated staff. Finding a better way to deliver services or making a difference in the lives of many people is often at the top of the list.

The main point is that success cannot be measured strictly by business profitability. However, if success is measured by the journey, and not just with statistics, the road map is much clearer and easier to follow. By maintaining their freedom and flexibility, women business owners can become truly creative and confident. And by providing an environment that cultivates respectful relationships, owners are able to focus on performance and profitability. This is not easy, but for women it is essential, and the rewards are definitely worth the effort.

The Disabled Entrepreneur

Those who succeed in their own business must be physically healthy and able-bodied in order to handle the long hours, stress, and physical demands associated with starting a business, right? Not really. In fact, an increasing number of people with disabilities and chronic health conditions are starting businesses, and are doing so at twice the rate of non-disabled persons!

Why are so many people with disabilities starting successful businesses each year? This trend may be due in part to the disastrously high unemployment rate among people with disabilities. According to the most recent figures available, people with disabilities are unemployed at a rate of about 70%! This figure is even more staggering when you consider the current economic boom where the rest of the population enjoys an unemployment rate of 2-5%.

People with disabilities and chronic health conditions choose to become self-employed for many reasons. Self-employment offers many the freedom to work at their own pace in an environment that accommodates their special needs. As a person with a disability or a chronic health condition, you may have tried unsuccessfully to find work or you may have found that your employer is unwilling or unable to accommodate your needs. You may be looking for an option that allows you to earn a living and manage your health at the same time. Owning a business often provides the flexibility that is necessary to those who require frequent medical attention, flexible hours, accessible workspace, or other special considerations.

Self-employment presents many challenges and it certainly is not for everyone. But for many people with disabilities and chronic health conditions, self-employment offers what may be their only hope of making a living and achieving self-sufficiency.

Several programs exist to assist people with disabilities. The U.S. Small Business Administration provides millions of dollars each year to support the initiatives for micro businesses. Check with the SBA office closest to you for more information about services available through the SBA. To reach that office either call 1-800-U-ASK-SBA or log on to www.sba.gov. The SBA has also announced a new initiative with the Department of Labor to develop programs for persons with disabilities.

In addition, state vocational rehabilitation programs provide a variety of services to aspiring entrepreneurs with disabilities. Each state has a vocational rehabilitation agency that serves free of charge all qualified individuals with disabilities. Vocational Rehabilitation programs were created to assist individuals in obtaining the skills, education, and resources needed to successfully join the workforce.

The Internet also provides a number of websites devoted to helping disabled people find the resources they need to support themselves. We have listed a number of good websites in Appendix A.

While challenging, self-employment has been successful for many disabled individuals. As more and more of the businesses they start succeed, this will become an important growth area of our economy. And, it is time. People who are disabled or have chronic health conditions have a lot to offer to the world. Their talents and skills have often been hidden. Through self-employment many will, hopefully, be able to take their place as leaders and contributors to economic growth.

The Hispanic Entrepreneur

In the 1980s, Hispanic Business functioned as both a validator and beneficiary of demographic change. The 1980 Census revealed 14.6 million Hispanics were living in the United States, a surge of 61 percent from the 9.07 million counted just 10 years before. Government, media, corporations, and the public abruptly became aware of the growing Hispanic middle class in their midst.

Politically, the 1980 Census meant more Hispanics in Congress. In 1981, Henry Cisneros became mayor of San Antonio. In 1985, Xavier Suarez became the first Cuban American to run Miami. Under the leadership of Jorge Mas Canosa, the Cuban American National Foundation exerted a strengthened influence in the Reagan administration. In 1989, Cuban-born Ileana Ros-Lehtinen became the first Hispanic woman elected to Congress. And, by the end of the decade, the first Bush administration had two Hispanics in the Cabinet, Education Secretary Lauro Cavazos and Interior Secretary Manuel Lujan.

A new category of print media catered to the new class of rising entrepreneurs. Magazines such as *Entrepreneur* (1973), *Inc.* (1979), and *Hispanic Business* (1979) began to document and celebrate the progress of small companies. The Hispanic Business 400 directory of companies debuted in 1983 and grew to 500 companies just two short years later.

In addition, Hispanic Business undertook a growing number of original research projects to document the burgeoning market, including the compilation of Hispanic media expenditures. The vital data added to a growing body of economic information about the Hispanic market coming from government agencies and academia's Chicano and Hispanic studies departments.

In the next decade, the U.S. economy would experience the longest run of prosperity on record, with Hispanic professionals and entrepreneurs positioned to take full advantage of it.

The Black Entrepreneur

Over the last two decades, black entrepreneurs have done more to improve the economic situation for "the black community" than any black pastor or politician. These entrepreneurs are taking the risks and building the businesses that create economic growth and prosperity. This is in stark contrast to the efforts of the Congressional Black Caucus, which has done little to encourage entrepreneurs and has limited its efforts to securing increased funding for feckless programs that harm African Americans. Sadly, many politically inclined black pastors are stuck in the rhetoric of the 1960s (and even the 1980s for that matter) speaking about the need for coercive affirmative action programs and lamenting the diminished economic status of African Americans.

And it is a surprise for many to learn that, according to research done by the Kaufman Foundation, blacks between the ages of 24 and 35 are 50% more likely than whites to engage in entrepreneurial activities. In other words, the most active group of entrepreneurs in American is black men and women. This reality, still waiting to be grasped by leaders in both political parties, is producing a new and welcome leadership paradigm in the black community.

According to a recent study by the Ewing Marion Kauffman Foundation, "blacks are starting companies at greater rates, but there is something within the process that causes them to fall out at greater rates."

Conclusion
The Future of Entrepreneurship

Entrepreneurs play a vital role in developing the economy. As important contributors to technological innovation and new job opportunities, entrepreneurs build communities by providing jobs, conducting business at a local level, creating and participating in entrepreneurial networks, investing in community projects, and by their philanthropic contributions. If we look at both the economic and social impact of entrepreneurship and how it has emerged in recent years, it is no surprise that many states and local communities have implemented sound strategies with the goal of cultivating and nurturing entrepreneurs.

As we all know, increasing numbers of people are electing to work from home either through telecommuting or by running a home-based business. While this trend has commonly been attributed to the growth in the number of working women wanting to be home for their children, quite a few men are staying home as well.

Therefore, if you have determined that entrepreneurship is for you, you can be confident that you are part of the wave of the future. But understand what it will demand and whether you are prepared to give what it will take. The appeal of entrepreneurship is undeniably strong for many but make sure you are going into it for the appropriate reasons. Being miserable in your job does not automatically make starting your own business the best idea in the world. In fact, it could be the worst reason of all to get into business and become your own boss. The right choice may instead be to find another job that satisfies your professional thirst and provides a pleasant environment for your creative juices. But if, after taking into account everything that you have read, you're adamant that you have what it takes, by all means get on the roller-coaster ride, fasten your seat belt and create something absolutely fabulous.

Final Thoughts

Lemonade stands are NOT just for kids anymore! If you are ready to turn lemons to lemonade; if you have the key ingredients to engineer your own flavor, and have the desire to nurture your business idea every step of the way, here are a few final thoughts for you:

- Get experience in the field before you break out on your own—you will have more credibility and will recognize the pitfalls to avoid

- If you lie, steal or cheat your customers, both the consumers *and* your competitors will find out

- Who you know is equally as important as what you know

- Be realistic in your expectations—don't give up when things don't happen as quickly as you would like

- *Network* everywhere you go—you never know where you might find a new customer or a great new idea

- Your most valuable possession is not your product, resources or wealth; it is your reputation

- Make sure your dreams are focused before you start

- Follow the philosophy of determination in everything you do

- Successful entrepreneurs need to focus on their customers, check their egos at the door, and avoid the paralysis of trying to make things perfect

- Even the best ideas can fail

- Entrepreneurship is all about passion…you need to feel the excitement.

Appendix A

Resources

❖

Available resources and publications for general information

Entrepreneurs with Disabilities
World Institute on Disabilities
http://www.wid.org/

The Entrepreneurs with Disabilities Network
http://www.entrepreneurdisability.org/

DisabilityInfo.gov
http://www.disabilityinfo.gov

Disabled Entrepreneurs Network
http://www.disabled-entrepreneurs.net

Minority Entrepreneur
Minority Business Development Agency
http://www.mbda.gov/

Women Entrepreneur
American Business
Women's Association
9100 Ward Parkway, PO Box 8728
Kansas City, MO 64114-0728

Phone (800) 228-0007
Fax (816) 361-4991

Business and Professional Women
1900 M Street, NW, Suite 310
Washington, D.C. 20036
Phone: (202) 293-1100
Fax: (202) 861-0298

Center for Women's Business Research
1411 K Street, NW, Suite 1350
Washington, DC 20005-3407
Phone: (202) 638-3060
Fax: (202) 638-3064

Office of Women's Business Ownership
Small Business Administration
409 Third Street SW, Fourth Floor
Washington, DC 20416
(202) 205-6673

National Association of Women Business Owners **(NAWBO)**
8405 Greensboro Drive
Suite 800
McLean VA 22102
Phone: (800) 55-NAWBO
Fax: (703) 506-3266

U.S. Department of Labor
Women's Bureau
200 Constitution Avenue, NW—Room S-3002
Washington, DC 20210
Telephone (800) 827-5335 or (202) 693-6710
Fax (202) 693-6725

Legal Information
US Department of Labor
E-Laws Advisors

http://www.dol.gov/elaws
Small Business Administration Publications
P.O. Box 46521
Denver, CO 80201-0030
(202) 205-6665
http://www.sba.gov

Government Printing Office
Superintendent of Documents
U.S. Government Printing Office
P.O. Box 371954
Pittsburg, PA 15250-7954
(866) 512-1800
http://bookstore.gpo.gov/index.html

Internal Revenue Service
Tax Information
(800) 829-1040
http://www.irs.gov

Department of Health and Human Services
Social Security Administration
(800) 772-1213
http://www.ssa/gov

Equal Employment Opportunity Commission
1801 L Street, N.W.
Washington, D.C. 20507
Phone: (202) 663-4900
TTY: (202) 663-4494
http://www.eeoc.gov

Federal Identification Number (Form SS-4)
(800) 829-3676

Federal Information Center
(800) 333-8636

Federal Reserve Bank
http://www.federalreserve.gov

Internal Revenue Service
(800) 829-1040
http://www.irs.gov

Occupational Safety and Health Administration
http://www.osha.gov

Patents and Trademark Information
Virginia (800) 786-9199

U.S. Census Bureau
Maryland (301) 457-4608

U.S. Copyright Information
Washington (202) 707-3000

U.S. Department of Commerce
Birmingham (205) 731-1331

U.S. Department of Labor, Wage/Hour Division
Birmingham (205) 731-1305

U.S. Forestry Department
(202) 205-1760

U.S. Small Business Administration
Birmingham (205) 290-7101

U.S. Veterans Administration
Montgomery (334) 213-3407

Resources by State

Small Business Administration

Alabama
Small Business Administration
Alabama District Office
801 Tom Martin Drive, Suite #201
Birmingham, AL 35211
Phone: (205) 290-7101
Fax: (205) 290-7404
http://www.sba.gov/al/

Alaska
Small Business Administration
Anchorage, AK District Office
510 L Street, Suite 310
Anchorage, AK 99501-1952
(907) 271-4022
http://www.sba.gov/regions/states/ak/

Arizona
Small Business Administration
Arizona District Office
2828 North Central Ave, Suite 800
Phoenix, Arizona 85004-1093
Telephone: (602) 745-7200
Facsimile: (602) 745-7210
http://www.sba.gov/az/

Arkansas
Small Business Administration
Arkansas District Office
2120 Riverfront Drive, Suite 250
Little Rock, AR 72202-1794
Telephone: (501) 324-5871
Facsimile: (501) 324-5199
http://www.sba.gov/ar/

California
Small Business Administration
Disaster Area 4 Office
P.O. Box 419004
Sacramento, CA 95841-9004
(800) 488-5323
Phone (916) 735-1500
TTY (916) 735-1683
Serving: Alaska, Washington, Oregon, Idaho, Nevada, California, Arizona, Hawaii, and Pacific Islands
http://www.sba.gov/disasterarea4/

Sacramento District Office
650 Capitol Mall, suite 7-500
Sacramento, CA 95814
(916) 930-3700 Phone
(916) 930-3737 Fax
http://www.sba.gov/ca/sacr/

San Francisco District Office
455 Market Street, 6th Floor
San Francisco, CA 94105-2420
(415) 744-6820
http://www.sba.gov/ca/sf/

Fresno District Office
2719 North Air Fresno Drive, Suite 200
Fresno, CA 93727
Phone: (559) 487-5791
Fax: (559) 487-5636
Toll free call (800) 359-1833 then press 6
http://www.sba.gov/ca/fresno/

Los Angeles District Office
330 North Brand, Suite 1200
Glendale, CA 91203
(818) 552-3215
http://www.sba.gov/ca/la/

Santa Ana District Office
200 W Santa Ana Blvd., Suite 700
Santa Ana, CA 92701
(714) 550-7420
TTY/TDD (714) 550-0655
Fax (714) 550-0191
http://www.sba.gov/ca/santa/

San Diego District Office
550 West "C" Street—Suite 550
San Diego, CA 92101-3500
(619) 557-7250
Fax (619) 557-5894
http://www.sba.gov/ca/sandiego/

Colorado
Small Business Administration
Colorado District Office
721 19th Street, Suite 426
Denver, CO 80202
(303) 844-2607
http://www.sba.gov/co/

Connecticut
Small Business Administration
Connecticut District Office
330 Main Street, Second Floor
Hartford, CT 06106
(860) 240-4700
http://www.sba.gov/ct/

Delaware
Small Business Administration
Wilmington, DE District Office
824 N. Market Street
Wilmington, DE 19801-3011
(302) 573-6294
http://www.sba.gov/de/

Florida
Small Business Administration
North Florida District Office
7825 Baymeadows Way, Suite 100B
Jacksonville, FL 32256-7504
(904) 443-1900
http://www.sba.gov/fl/north/

South Florida District Office
100 S. Biscayne Blvd—7th Floor
Miami, FL 33131
(305) 536-5521
Fax (305)536-5058
http://www.sba.gov/fl/south/

Georgia
Small Business Administration
Georgia District Office
233 Peachtree Street, NE, Suite 1900
Atlanta, GA 30303
(404) 331-0100
http://www.sba.gov/ga/

Hawaii
Small Business Administration
Hawaii District Office
300 Ala Moana Blvd
Room 2-235
Box 50207
Honolulu, Hawaii 96850
Phone (808) 541-2990
Fax (808) 541-2976
http://www.sba.gov/hi/

Idaho
Small Business Administration
Boise District Office
380 East Parkcenter Blvd., Suite 330

Boise, Idaho 83706
Phone: (208) 334-1696
Fax: (208) 334-9353
http://www.sba.gov/id/

Illinois
Small Business Administration
Illinois District Office
500 W. Madison Street, Suite 1250
Chicago, Illinois 60661-2511
(312) 353-4528
http://www.sba.gov/il/

Indiana
Small Business Administration
Indiana District Office
429 North Pennsylvania Street, Suite 100
Indianapolis, IN 46204-1873
(317) 226-7272
http://www.sba.gov/in/

Iowa
Small Business Administration
Des Moines District Office
210 Walnut St, Rm 749
Des Moines, IA 50309
(515) 284-4422
http://www.sba.gov/ia/desmo/

Cedar Rapids Branch Office
215 4th Ave SE, Suite 200
Cedar Rapids, IA 52401
(319) 362-6405
http://www.sba.gov/ia/cedar/

Kansas
Small Business Administration
Kansas District Office

271 W 3rd ST, N STE 2500
Wichita, KS 67202
(316) 269-6616
http://www.sba.gov/ks/

Kentucky
Small Business Administration
Kentucky District Office
600 Dr. MLK Jr. PL
Louisville, KY 40202
(502) 582-5971
http://www.sba.gov/ky/

Louisiana
Small Business Administration
New Orleans District Office
365 Canal St., Suite 2820
New Orleans, LA 70130
(504) 589-6685
http://www.sba.gov/la/

Maine
Small Business Administration
Maine District Office
Edmund S. Muskie Federal Building, Room 512
68 Sewall Street
Augusta, ME 04330
(207) 622-8274
http://www.sba.gov/me/

Maryland
Small Business Administration
Maryland District Office
City Crescent Building, 6th Floor
10 South Howard Street
Baltimore, Maryland 21201
(410) 962-4392
http://www.sba.gov/md/

Massachusetts
Small Business Administration
Massachusetts District Office
10 Causeway Street, Room 265
Boston, MA 02222
(617) 565-5590
http://www.sba.gov/ma/

Michigan
Small Business Administration
Michigan District Office
477 Michigan Avenue
Suite 515, McNamara Building
Detroit, Michigan 48226
(313) 226-6075
http://www.sba.gov/mi/

Minnesota
Small Business Administration
Minneapolis, MN District Office
100 North Sixth Street
Suite 210-C Butler Square
Minneapolis, Minnesota 55403
(612) 370-2324
(612) 370-2303
http://www.sba.gov/mn/

Mississippi
Small Business Administration
Mississippi District Office
AmSouth Bank Plaza
210 E. Capitol Street, Suite 900
Jackson, Mississippi 39201
(601) 965-4378
Fax: (601) 965-5629
     (601) 965-4294

Gulfport Branch Office
Hancock Bank Plaza
2510 14th Street, Suite 101
Gulfport, MS 39501
(228) 863-4449
Fax: (228) 864-0179
http://www.sba.gov/ms/

Missouri

Small Business Administration
Kansas City District Office
323 W 8th St. Suite 501
Kansas City, MO 64105
(816) 374-6701
http://www.sba.gov/mo/kansas/

Eastern Missouri District Office
200 North Broadway, Suite 1500
St. Louis, MO 63102
(314) 539-6600
Fax: (314) 539-3785
http://www.sba.gov/mo/stlouis/

Montana

Small Business Administration
Montana District Office
10 West 15th Street Suite 1100
Helena, MT 59626
(406) 441-1081
Fax: (406) 441-1090
http://www.sba.gov/mt/

Nebraska

Small Business Administration
Nebraska District Office
11145 Mill Valley Rd.
Omaha, NE 68154

(402) 221-4691
http://www.sba.gov/ne/

Nevada
Small Business Administration
Nevada District Office
400 South 4th Street, Suite 250
Las Vegas, NV 89101
(702) 388-6611
Fax: (702) 388-6469
http://www.sba.gov/nv/

New Hampshire
Small Business Administration
New Hampshire District Office
JC Cleveland Federal Building
55 Pleasant Street, Suite 3101
Concord, NH 03301
(603) 225-1400
Fax: (603) 225-1409
http://www.sba.gov/nh/

New Jersey
Small Business Administration
New Jersey District Office
Two Gateway Center, 15th Floor
Newark, New Jersey 07102
(973) 645-2434
http://www.sba.gov/nj/

New Mexico
Small Business Administration
Albuquerque District Office
625 Silver SW, Suite 320
Albuquerque, NM 87102
(505) 346-7909
Fax (505) 346-6711
http://www.sba.gov/nm/

New York
Small Business Administration
Syracuse District Office
401 S. Salina Street 5th Floor
Syracuse, New York 13202
(315) 471-9393
Fax (315) 471-9288
http://www.sba.gov/ny/syracuse/

Disaster Area 1 Office
360 Rainbow Blvd., South
Niagara Falls, N.Y. 14303
(800) 659-2955
(716) 282-4612
Serving: Rhode Island, Pennsylvania, W. Virginia, Virginia, D.C., Connecticut,
New Jersey, Delaware, Maryland, Puerto Rico, and U.S. Virgin Islands
http://www.sba.gov/disasterarea1/

Buffalo District Office
111 West Huron Street, Suite 1311
Buffalo, New York 14202
(716) 551-4301
Fax (716) 551-4418
http://www.sba.gov/ny/buffalo/

New York District Office
26 Federal Plaza, Suite 3100
New York, NY 10278
(212) 264-4354
Fax (212) 264-4963
http://www.sba.gov/ny/ny/

SBA REGION II Office
26 Federal Plaza, Suite 3108
New York, NY 10278
(212) 264-1450
Serving: New York, New Jersey, Puerto Rico, and U.S. Virgin Islands
http://www.sba.gov/region2/

North Carolina

Small Business Administration
North Carolina District Office
6302 Fairview Road, Suite 300
Charlotte, NC 28210
(704) 344-6563
Fax (704) 344-6769
http://www.sba.gov/nc/

North Dakota

Small Business Administration
North Dakota District Office
657 Second Avenue North, Room 219
Fargo, ND 58102
(701) 239-5131
http://www.sba.gov/nd/

Ohio

Small Business Administration
Cleveland, OH District Office
1111 Superior Avenue, Suite 630
Cleveland, OH 44114-2507
(216) 522-4180
Fax: (216) 522-2038
TDD: (216) 522-8350
http://www.sba.gov/oh/cleveland/

Columbus, OH District Office
Two Nationwide Plaza, Suite 1400
Columbus, Ohio 43215
(614) 469-6860
http://www.sba.gov/oh/columbus/

Columbus, OH District Office
Two Nationwide Plaza, Suite 1400
Columbus, Ohio 43215
(614) 469-6860
http://www.sba.gov/oh/columbus/

Oklahoma
Small Business Administration
Oklahoma City District Office
Federal Building
301 NW 6th St
Oklahoma City, OK 73102
(405) 609-8000
http://www.sba.gov/ok/

Oregon
Small Business Administration
Portland, OR District Office
1515 SW 5th Avenue, Suite 1050
Portland, Oregon 97201-5494
(503) 326-2682
Fax: (503) 326-2808
http://www.sba.gov/or/

Pennsylvania
Small Business Administration
Pittsburgh District Office
Federal Building—Room 1128
1000 Liberty Avenue
Pittsburgh, PA 15222
(412) 395-6560
http://www.sba.gov/pa/pitt/

Philadelphia District Office
Robert N.C. Nix Federal Building
900 Market Street, 5th Floor
Philadelphia, PA 19107
(215) 580-2SBA
http://www.sba.gov/pa/phil/

Rhode Island
Small Business Administration
Rhode Island District Office
380 Westminster Street, Room 511

Providence, RI 02903
(401) 528-4561
http://www.sba.gov/ri/

South Carolina

Small Business Administration
South Carolina District Office
1835 Assembly Street, Room 358
Columbia, South Carolina 29201
(803) 765-5377
Fax (803) 765-5962
http://www.sba.gov/sc/

South Dakota

Small Business Administration
South Dakota District Office
2329 N. Career Ave., Suite 105
Sioux Falls, SD 57107
(605) 330-4243
Fax: (605) 330-4215
TTY/TDD: (605) 331-3527
http://www.sba.gov/sd/

Tennessee

Small Business Administration
Tennessee District Office
50 Vantage Way, Suite 201
Nashville, TN 37228
(615) 736-5881 Phone
Fax (615) 736-7232
TTY/TDD (615) 736-2499
http://www.sba.gov/tn/

Texas

Small Business Administration
Lubbock District Office
1205 Texas Avenue, Room 408
Lubbock, TX. 79401-2693

(806) 472-7462
Fax: (806) 472-7487
http://www.sba.gov/tx/lubbock/

El Paso District Office
10737 Gateway West
El Paso, TX 79935
(915) 633-7001
Fax (915) 633-7005
http://www.sba.gov/tx/elpaso/

Harlingen District Office
222 East Van Buren Street, Suite 500
Harlingen, TX 78550
(956) 427-8533
http://www.sba.gov/tx/harlingen/

Corpus Christi Branch Office
3649 Leopard Street, Suite 411
Corpus Christi, TX 78408
(361) 879-0017

Houston District Office
8701 S. Gessner Drive, Suite 1200
Houston, Texas 77074
(713) 773-6500
Fax (713) 773-6550
http://www.sba.gov/tx/hous/

San Antonio District Office
17319 San Pedro, Suite 200
(210) 403-5900
Fax: (210) 403-5936
TDD: (210) 403-5933
http://www.sba.gov/tx/sanantonio/

SBA Region VI Office
Dallas Regional Office

4300 Amon Carter Boulevard Suite 108
Fort Worth, TX 76155
(817) 684-5581
Fax (817) 684-5588
TTY/TDD (817) 684-5552
Serving: New Mexico, Texas, Oklahoma, Louisiana, and Arkansas
http://www.sba.gov/region6/

Utah
Small Business Administration
Utah District Office
125 South State Street, Room 2231
Salt Lake City, UT 84138
(801) 524-3209
http://www.sba.gov/ut/

Vermont
Small Business Administration
Vermont District Office
87 State Street, Room 205
Montpelier, VT 05601
(802) 828-4422
http://www.sba.gov/vt/

Virginia
Small Business Administration
Richmond, VA District Office
400 North 8th Street
Federal Bldg., Suite 1150
Richmond, VA 23240
(804) 771-2400
http://www.sba.gov/va/

Washington
Small Business Administration
Seattle, WA District Office
1200 Sixth Avenue, Suite 1700
Corner of Sixth and University

Seattle, WA 98101-1128
(206) 553-7310
http://www.sba.gov/wa/seattle/

Spokane, WA Branch Office
801 W. Riverside Avenue, Suite 200
Spokane, WA 99201
(509) 353-2800
http://www.sba.gov/wa/spokane/

West Virginia
Small Business Administration
West Virginia District Office
320 West Pike Street, Suite 330
Clarksburg, WV 26301
(304) 623-5631
http://www.sba.gov/wv/

Wisconsin
Small Business Administration
Wisconsin District Office
740 Regent Street, Suite 100
Madison, WI 53715
(608) 441-5263
Fax (608) 441-5541
http://www.sba.gov/wi/

310 West Wisconsin Ave. Room 400
Milwaukee, WI 53203
(414) 297-3941
Fax (414) 297-1377

Wyoming
Small Business Administration
Wyoming District Office
100 East B Street, Federal Building
P.O. Box 2839
Casper, Wyoming 82602

(307) 261-6500
http://www.sba.gov/wy/

Guam
Small Business Administration
Guam Branch Office
400 Route 8, Suite 302
First Hawaiian Bank Building
Mongmong, GU 96927
(671) 472-7419
Fax (671) 472-7365
http://www.sba.gov/gu/

Puerto Rico & U.S. Virgin Islands
Small Business Administration
Puerto Rico and US Virgin Islands District Office
252 Ponce de Leon Ave.
Citibank Tower, Suite 201
Hato Rey, PR 00918
(787) 766-5572
(800) 669-8049
Fax (787) 766-5309
http://www.sba.gov/pr/

Better Business Bureau

Alabama
WWW: http://www.birmingham-al.bbb.org
Email: info@birmingham-al.bbb.org
Phone: (205) 558-2222
Fax: (205) 558-2239
PO Box 55268
Birmingham, AL 35255-5268

Alaska
WWW: http://www.alaska.bbb.org
Email: info@anchorage.bbb.org
Phone: (907) 562-0704
Fax: (907) 562-4061
719 E 11th
Anchorage, AK 99501-4613

Arizona
WWW: http://www.phoenix.bbb.org
Email: info@phoenix.bbb.org
Phone: (602) 264-1721
Fax: (602) 263-0997
4428 N. 12th Street
Phoenix, AZ 85014-4585

Arkansas
WWW: http://www.arkansas.bbb.org
Email: info@bbbarkansas.org
Phone: (501) 664-7274
Fax: (501) 664-0024
12521 Kanis Road
Little Rock, AR 72211-2605

California
Southland
WWW: http://www.labbb.org
Email: info@labbb.org

Phone: (909) 825-7280
Fax: (909) 825-6246
PO Box 970
Colton, CA 92324-3052

San Diego
WWW: http://www.sandiego.bbb.org
Email: info@sandiego.bbb.org
Phone: (858) 496-2131
Fax: (858) 496-2141
5050 Murphy Canyon, Ste. 110
San Diego, CA 92123

Oakland
WWW: http://www.oakland.bbb.org
Email: info@oakland.bbb.org
Phone: (510) 238-1000
Fax: (510) 238-1018
510 16th Street, Ste. 550
Oakland, CA 94612-1584

Colorado
Denver Area
WWW: http://www.denver.bbb.org
Email: info@denver.bbb.org
Phone: (303) 758-2100
Fax: (303) 758-8321
1020 Cherokee Street
Denver, CO 80204-4039

Connecticut
WWW: http://www.connecticut.bbb.org
Email: info@ctbbb.org
Phone: (203) 269-2700
Fax: (203) 269-3124
821 N. Main Street Ext. Parkside Building
Wallingford, CT 06492-2420

Delaware
WWW: http://www.delaware.bbb.org
Email: info@delaware.bbb.org
Phone: (302) 230-0108
Fax: (302) 230-0116
1415 Foulk Road, Suite 202
Foulkstone Plaza
Wilmington, DE 19803

District of Columbia
Metro Washington DC and Eastern Pennsylvania
WWW: http://www.dc.bbb.org
Email: info@dc.bbb.org
Phone: (202) 393-8000
Fax: (202) 393-1198
1411 K St., NW, 10th Floor
Washington, DC 20005-3404

Florida
Miami, Ft. Lauderdale, and West Palm Beach Areas
WWW: http://www.bbbsoutheastflorida.org
Email: info@seflorida.bbb.org
Phone: (561) 842-1918
Fax: (561) 845-7234
2924 N Australian Ave.
West Palm Beach, FL 33407

Northeast Florida
WWW: http://www.bbbnefla.org
Email: info@bbbnefla.org
Phone: (904) 721-2288
Fax: (904) 721-7373
4417 Beach BV., Suite 202
Jacksonville, FL 32207

Georgia
Metro Atlanta, Athens & Northeast Georgia
WWW: http://www.atlanta.bbb.org

Email: info@atlanta.bbb.org
Phone: (404) 766-0875
Fax: (404) 768-1085
503 Oak Place, Suite 590
Atlanta, GA 30349

Hawaii
WWW: http://www.hawaii.bbb.org
Email: info@hawaii.bbb.org
Phone: (808) 536-6956
Fax: (808) 523-2335
First Hawaiian Tower; 1132 Bishop Street, Ste. 1507
Honolulu, HI 96813-2822

Idaho
Southwest Idaho
WWW: http://www.boise.bbb.org
Email: info@boise.bbb.org
Phone: (208) 342-4649
Fax: (208) 342-5116
4355 Emerald St., Suite 290
Boise, ID 83706

Illinois
Chicago and N. Illinois
WWW: http://www.chicago.bbb.org
Email: feedback@chicago.bbb.org
Phone: (312) 832-0500
Fax: (312) 832-9985
330 N. Wabash, Ste. 2006
Chicago, IL 60611

Indiana
Central Indiana
WWW: http://www.indybbb.org
Email: info@central-in.bbb.org
Phone: (317) 488-2222
Fax: (317) 488-2224

Victoria Centre 22 E. Washington St., Ste. 200
Indianapolis, IN 46204-3584

Iowa
Central & Eastern Iowa
WWW: http://www.desmoines.bbb.org
Email: info@dm.bbb.org
Phone: (515) 243-8137
Fax: (515) 243-2227
505 5th Ave., Ste. 950
Des Moines, IA 50309-2375

Kansas
WWW: http://www.wichita.bbb.org
Email: info@wichita.bbb.org
Phone: (316) 263-3146
Fax: (316) 263-3063
328 Laura
Wichita, KS 67211-1707

Kentucky
WWW: http://www.ky-in.bbb.org
Email: info@ky-in.bbb.org
Phone: (502) 583-6546
Fax: (502) 589-9940
844 S. 4th Street
Louisville, KY 40203-2186

Louisiana
Greater New Orleans Area
WWW: http://www.neworleans.bbb.org
Email: info@neworleans.bbb.org
Phone: (504) 581-6222
Fax: (504) 524-9110
1539 Jackson Ave., Ste. 400
New Orleans, LA 70130-5843

South Central Louisiana
WWW: http://www.batonrouge.bbb.org
Email: jims@batonrouge.bbb.org
Phone: (225) 346-5222
Fax: (225) 346-1029
748 Main Street
Baton Rouge, LA 70802

Maine
WWW: http://www.bosbbb.org
Email: info@bosbbb.org
Phone: (207) 878-2715
Fax: (207) 797-5818
812 Stevens Ave.
Portland, ME 04103-2648

Maryland
WWW: http://www.baltimore.bbb.org
Email: info@bbbmd.org
Phone: (410) 347-3992
Fax: (410) 347-3936
1414 Key Highway, Suite 100
Baltimore, MD 21230-5189

Massachusetts
Eastern Massachusetts, Maine & Vermont
WWW: http://www.bosbbb.org
Email: info@bosbbb.org
Phone: (508) 652-4800
Fax: (508) 652-4820
235 West Central Street, Suite 1
Natick, MA 01760-3767

Michigan
Detroit & Eastern Michigan
WWW: http://www.easternmichiganbbb.org
Email: info@easternmichiganbbb.org
Phone: (248) 644-9100

Fax: (248) 644-5026
30555 Southfield Road, Ste. 200
Southfield, MI 48076-7751

Minnesota
WWW: http://www.mnd.bbb.org
Email: ask@mnd.bbb.org
Phone: (651) 699-1111
Fax: (651) 699-7665
2706 Gannon Road
Saint Paul, MN 55116-2600

Mississippi
WWW: http://www.bbbmississippi.org
Email: info@bbbmississippi.org
Phone: (601) 977-1020
Fax: (601) 977-0704
P.O. Box 3302
Ridgeland, MS 39158

Missouri
E. Missouri and S. Illinois
WWW: http://www.stlouis.bbb.org
Email: bbbstl@stlouisbbb.org
Phone: (314) 645-3300
Fax: (314) 645-2666
12 Sunnen Drive, Ste. 121
Saint Louis, MO 63143

Montana
Eastern Washington, North Idaho and Montana
WWW: http://www.thelocalbbb.com
Email: info@thelocalbbb.com
Phone: (509) 455-4200
Fax: (509) 838-1079
508 West Sixth Avenue, Ste. 401
Spokane, WA 99204-2356

Nebraska
WWW: http://www.lincoln.bbb.org
Phone: (402) 436-2345
Fax: (402) 476-8221
3633 O Street, Ste. 1
Lincoln, NE 68510-1670

Nevada
Southern Nevada
WWW: http://www.vegasbbb.org
Email: scampbell@vegasbbb.org
Phone: (702) 320-4500
Fax: (702) 320-4560
2301 Palomino Lane
Las Vegas, NV 89107-4503

Northern Nevada, Inc.
WWW: http://www.renobbb.org
Email: information@renobbb.org
Phone: (775) 322-0657
Fax: (775) 322-8163
991 Bible Way
Reno, NV 89502-2122

New Hampshire
WWW: http://www.concord.bbb.org
Email: info@bbbnh.org
Phone: (603) 224-1991
Fax: (603) 228-9035
410 S. Main Street
Concord, NH 03301-3483

New Jersey
WWW: http://www.trenton.bbb.org
Email: info@trenton.bbb.org
Phone: (609) 588-0808
Fax: (609) 588-0546

1700 Whitehorse Hamilton Square, Ste. D-5
Trenton, NJ 08690-3596

New Mexico
WWW: http://www.bbbnm.com
Email: bureau@bbbnm.com
Phone: (505) 346-0110
Fax: (505) 346-0696
2625 Pennsylvania NE, Ste. 2050
Albuquerque, NM 87110-3657

New York
Metropolitan New York
WWW: http://www.newyork.bbb.org
Email: inquiry@newyork.bbb.org
Phone: (212) 533-6200
Fax: (212) 477-4912
257 Park Avenue South
New York, NY 10010-7384

Long Island
WWW: http://www.newyork.bbb.org
Email: longisland@newyork.bbb.org
Phone: (212) 533-6200
Fax: (516) 420-1095
399 Conklin St
Farmingdale, NY 11735-2618

Mid-Hudson
WWW: http://www.newyork.bbb.org
Email: mhinquiries@newyork.bbb.org
Phone: (212) 533-6200
Fax: (914) 428-6030
99 Lafayette Avenue
White Plains, NY 10603-3213

North Carolina
Eastern North Carolina, Inc.

WWW: http://www.bbbenc.org
Email: info@raleigh.bbb.org
Phone: (919) 277-4222
Fax: (919) 277-4221
5540 Munford Road, Suite 130
Raleigh, NC 27612-2621

Asheville/Western NC
WWW: http://www.asheville.bbb.org
Email: info@asheville.bbb.org
Phone: (828) 253-2392
Fax: (828) 252-5039
One West Pack Square, Suite 1601
Asheville, NC 28801-3408

Southern Piedmont
WWW: http://www.charlotte.bbb.org
Email: info@charlotte.bbb.org
Phone: (704) 527-0012
Fax: (704) 525-7624
5200 Park Road, Ste. 202
Charlotte, NC 28209-3650

North Carolina
WWW: http://www.nwnc.bbb.org
Email: bbb@nwncbbb.com
Phone: (336) 725-8348
Fax: (336) 777-3727
500 W. 5th St., Ste. 202
Winston Salem, NC 27101-2728

North Dakota
WWW: http://www.mnd.bbb.org
Email: ask@mnd.bbb.org
Phone: (651) 699-1111
Fax: (651) 699-7665
2706 Gannon Road
Saint Paul, MN 55116-2600

Ohio
Cleveland
WWW: http://www.cleveland.bbb.org
Email: info@cleveland.bbb.org
Phone: (216) 241-7678
Fax: (216) 861-6365
2217 E. 9th Street, Ste. 200
Cleveland, OH 44115-1299

Cincinnati
WWW: http://www.cinbbb.org
Email: info@cinbbb.org
Phone: (513) 421-3015
Fax: (513) 621-0907
898 Walnut Street
Cincinnati, OH 45202-2097

Oklahoma
Central Oklahoma
WWW: http://www.oklahomacity.bbb.org
Email: info@oklahomacity.bbb.org
Phone: (405) 239-6081
Fax: (405) 235-5891
17 S. Dewey
Oklahoma City, OK 73102-2400

Oregon
Oregon and Western Washington
WWW: http://www.thebbb.org
Email: info@thebbb.org
Phone: (503) 226-3981
Fax: (503) 226-8200
333 SW Fifth Ave., Ste. 406
Portland, OR 97204

Pennsylvania
Western Pennsylvania
WWW: http://www.pittsburgh.bbb.org

Email: info@pittsburgh.bbb.org
Phone: (412) 456-2700
Fax: (412) 456-2739
300 Sixth Avenue, Ste. 100-UL
Pittsburgh, PA 15222-2511

Metro Washington DC and Eastern Pennsylvania
WWW: http://www.easternpa.bbb.org
Email: info@philadelphia.bbb.org
Phone: (215) 85-9313
Fax: (215) 893-9312
1608 Walnut Street, Ste. 600
Philadelphia, PA 19103-0297

Rhode Island
WWW: http://www.rhodeisland.bbb.org
Email: info@rhodeisland.bbb.org
Phone: (401) 785-1212
Fax: (401) 785-3061
120 Lavan Street
Warwick, RI 02888-1071

South Carolina
WWW: http://www.columbia.bbb.org
Email: info@columbia.bbb.org
Phone: (803) 254-2525
Fax: (803) 779-3117
PO Box 8326
Columbia, SC 29202

South Dakota
Better Business Bureau, Inc.
WWW: http://www.heartlandbbb.org
Email: info@heartlandbbb.org
Phone: (402) 391-7612
Fax: (402) 391-7535
11811 P Street
Omaha, NE 68137

Tennessee
Greater East Tennessee
WWW: http://www.knoxville.bbb.org
Email: info@knoxville.bbb.org
Phone: (865) 692-1600
Fax: (865) 692-1590
PO Box 31377
Knoxville, TN 37930

Nashville/Middle Tennessee
WWW: http://www.middletennessee.bbb.org
Email: bbbnash@aol.com
Phone: (615) 242-4222
Fax: (615) 50-4245
PO Box 198436
Nashville, TN 37219-8436

Texas
Metropolitan Dallas
WWW: http://www.dallas.bbb.org
Email: info@dallas.bbb.org
Phone: (214) 220-2000
Fax: (214) 740-0321
1600 Pacific, Suite 2800
Dallas, TX 75201

Metropolitan Houston
WWW: http://www.bbbhou.org
Email: bbbinfo@bbbhou.org
Phone: (713) 341-6167
Fax: (713) 867-4947
1333 West Loop South, Suite 1200
Houston, TX 77027

El Paso
WWW: http://www.bbbelpaso.com
Phone: (915) 577-0191
Fax: (915) 577-0209

221 N. Kansas, Ste. 1101
El Paso, TX 79901

Coastal Bend
WWW: http://www.caller.com/bbb
Phone: (361) 852-4949
Fax: (361) 852-4990
4301 Ocean Drive
Corpus Christi, TX 78412

Utah
WWW: http://www.utah.bbb.org
Email: info@utah.bbb.org
Phone: (801) 892-6009
Fax: (801) 892-6002
5673 S. Redwood Rd., #22
Salt Lake City, UT 84123-5322

Vermont
Eastern Massachusetts, Maine & Vermont
WWW: http://www.bosbbb.org
Email: info@bosbbb.org
Phone: (508) 652-4800
Fax: (508) 652-4820
235 West Central Street, Suite 1
Natick, MA 01760-3767

Virginia
Central Virginia
WWW: http://www.richmond.bbb.org
Email: info@richmond.bbb.org
Phone: (804) 648-0016
Fax: (804) 648-3115
701 E. Franklin, Ste. 712
Richmond, VA 23219-2332

Greater Hampton Roads
WWW: http://www.norfolk.bbb.org

Email: info@hamptonroadsbbb.org
Phone: (757) 531-1300
Fax: (757) 531-1388
586 Virginian Drive
Norfolk, VA 23505

Washington
Oregon and Western Washington
WWW: http://www.thebbb.org
Email: info@thebbb.org
Phone: (206) 431-2222
Fax: (206) 431-2211
PO Box 1000
DuPont, WA 98327

Eastern Washington, North Idaho and Montana
WWW: http://www.thelocalbbb.com
Email: info@thelocalbbb.com
Phone: (509) 455-4200
Fax: (509) 838-1079
508 West Sixth Avenue, Ste. 401
Spokane, WA 99204-2356

West Virginia
BBB/Canton Regional
WWW: http://www.cantonbbb.org
Email: info@cantonbbb.org
Phone: (800) 362-0494
Fax: (330) 456-8957
PO Box 8017
Canton, OH 44711-8017

Wisconsin
WWW: http://www.wisconsin.bbb.org
Email: info@wisconsin.bbb.org
Phone: (414) 847-6000
Fax: (414) 302-0355

10101 W. Greenfield Avenue, Suite 125
West Allis, WI 53214

Wyoming
WWW: http://www.fortcollins.bbb.org
Email: info@rockymtn.bbb.org
Phone: (970) 484-1348
Fax: (970) 221-1239
1730 S. College Ave., #303
Fort Collins, CO 80525

Federal Reserve Banks

California
101 Market Street
San Francisco, CA 94105
(415) 974-2000

Georgia
1000 Peachtree Street, NE
Atlanta, GA 30309-4470
(404) 498-8500

Illinois
230 South LaSalle Street
Chicago, IL 60604
(312) 322-5322

Massachusetts
600 Atlantic Avenue
Boston, MA 02106
(617) 973-3000

Minnesota
90 Hennepin Avenue
P.O. Box 291
Minneapolis, MN 55480-0291
(612) 204-5000

Missouri
925 Grand Boulevard
Kansas City, MO 64198
(816) 881-2000

411 Locust Street
St. Louis, MO 63102
(314) 444-8444

New York
33 Liberty Street
New York, NY 10045
(212) 720-5000

Ohio
1455 East Sixth Street
Cleveland, OH 44114
(216) 579-2000

Pennsylvania
Ten Independence Mall
Philadelphia, PA 19106
(215) 574-6000

Texas
2200 North Pearl Street
Dallas, TX 75201
(214) 922-6000

Virginia
701 East Byrd Street
Richmond, VA 23219
(804) 697-8000

Tax Information

Alabama
Department of Revenue
Gordon Persons Building
50 N. Ripley Street
Montgomery, AL 36132
(334) 242-1170

Alaska
Department of Revenue
333 W. Willoughby Ave., 11th Floor Side B
P.O. Box 110420
Juneau, AK 99811-0420
(907) 465-2320
http://www.state.ak.us

Arizona
Department of Revenue
1600 W. Monroe
Phoenix, AZ 85007
(602) 255-3381
(800) 352-4090

Arkansas
Office of Income Tax Administration
Joel Y. Ledbetter Building
Little Rock, AK 72201
(501) 682-1130
(501) 682-7751 Problem Resolution Office

California
Secretary of State General Information: (916) 653-6814
Corporations Unit: (916) 657-5488

State Franchise Tax Board
Taxpayer Assistance: (800) 400-7115
Taxpayers' Right Advocate: (888) 324-2798

Colorado
Department of Revenue
1375 Sherman St.
Denver, CO 80261
(303) 232-2446

Connecticut
Department of Revenue Services
25 Sigourney Street
Hartford, CT 06106-5032
Taxpayer Services (800) 382-9463 (in-state)
Taxpayer Services (800) 297-5962 (out-of-state)

Delaware
State of Delaware
Division of Corporations
401 Federal Street, Suite 4
Dover, Delaware 19901
(302) 739-3073

Delaware Division of Revenue
820 N. French Street
Wilmington, DE 19801
(302) 577-8205
http://www.state.de.us/revenue

District of Columbia
OTR Customer Service Center
941 North Capitol Street, NE
Washington, DC 20002
(202) 727-4829

Florida
Department of Revenue
Tax Information Services
1379 Blountstown Highway
Tallahassee, FL 32304-2716

Taxpayer Services: (850) 488-6800
(800) 352-3671 (in Florida only)

Georgia
Secretary of State Corporate Division
2 MLK Dr. S.E.
Suite 315, West Tower
Atlanta, GA 30334
(404) 656-2817

Georgia Department of Revenue Headquarters:
1800 Century Center Blvd., N.E.
Atlanta, GA 30345-3205
(404) 417-2300

Hawaii
Taxpayer Services Branch
P.O. Box 259
Honolulu, HI 96809
(808) 587-4242
(808) 587-6515 (Jan.–Apr. 20)
(800) 222-3229 (Toll-Free)

Idaho
State Tax Commission
P.O. Box 56
Boise, ID 83707-0076
(800) 972-7660

Office of the Secretary of State
700 W Jefferson, Room 203
P.O. Box 83720
Boise ID 83720-0080
(208) 334-2300

Illinois
Secretary of State Business Services
(217) 782-6961 (Springfield)
(312) 793-3380 (Chicago)

Department of Revenue
101 W. Jefferson St.
Springfield, IL 62702
(217) 782-3336
(800) 732-8866
http://www.revenue.state.il.us

Indiana
Secretary of State Business Services Division
(317) 232-6576
Department of Revenue
100 N. Senate Ave.
Indianapolis, IN 46204
(317) 232-2240

Iowa
Department of Revenue and Finance
Taxpayer Services/4th Floor
1305 E. Walnut
Des Moines, Iowa 50319
(515) 281-3114

The Secretary of State Business Services Division
Lucas Building, 1st Floor
Des Moines, IA 50319
(515) 281-5204

Kansas
Department of Revenue
Docking State Office Building, Room 150
915 SW Harrison St.
Topeka, KS 66612

(785) 368-8222
(877) 526-7738

The Kansas Secretary of State
Memorial Hall, 1st Floor
120 SW 10th Ave.
Topeka, KS 66612-1594
(785) 296-4564

Kentucky
Revenue Cabinet
200 Fair Oaks Lane
Frankfurt, KY 40620
(502) 564-4581 General Information
(502) 564-7822 Taxpayer Ombudsman
(502) 564-5572 Business Tax Branch

The Secretary of State Business Filings Office
700 Capitol Avenue
Room 154, State Capitol
P.O. Box 718
Frankfort, KY 40602
(502) 564-2848

Louisiana
Department of Revenue and Taxation
P.O. Box 201
Baton Rouge, LA 70821
(225) 219-2200 Taxpayer Services
(225) 219-0102 Personal Income Tax
(225) 219-0067 Corporate and Franchise Tax

Maine
Revenue Services
24 State House Station
Augusta, ME 04333-0024
(207) 287-2076

Maryland
Comptroller of Maryland
Revenue Administration Division
Revenue Administration Center
Annapolis MD 21411-0001
(410) 260-7980
(800) MD-TAXES

The State Department of Assessments and Taxation
301 W. Preston St.
Baltimore, MD 21201
(410) 767-1184

Massachusetts
Department of Revenue
P.O. Box 7010
Boston, MA 02204
200 Arlington St.
(617) 887-MDOR
(800) 392-6089

Michigan
Department of Treasury
Treasury Building
430 West Allegan Street
Lansing, MI 48922
(800) 487-7000 Income tax division
(517) 373-3200 General information

Department of Commerce's Corporation Division
Bureau of Commercial Services
Corporation Division
P.O. Box 30054
Lansing, MI 48909
(517) 241-6470

Minnesota
Department of Revenue

600 North Robert St.
St. Paul, MN 55146
(651) 296-3781
(800) 652-9094
(651) 296-0992 Taxpayer Rights Advocate

The Department of Revenue Business Services Department
(651) 296-2803
(877) 551-6SOS (6767)

Mississippi
State Tax Commission
P.O. Box 1033
Jackson, MS 39215-1033
(601) 923-7000

Missouri
Department of Revenue
Division of Taxation & Collection
2510 South Brentwood, Suite 300
Brentwood, MO 63144
(314) 301-1660 (business taxes)
(314) 301-1690 (income taxes)

Montana
Department of Revenue
P.O. Box 5805
Helena, MT 59604-5805
(406) 444-6900 Customer Service Center

Nebraska
Department of Revenue
301 Centennial Mall South, 2nd Floor
Taxpayer Assistance
P.O. Box 94818
Lincoln, NE 68509-4818
(800) 742-7474
(402) 471-5729

The Secretary of State Corporations Division
Room 1305
State Capitol
P.O. Box 94608
Lincoln, NE 68509-4608
(402) 471-4079

Nevada
Department of Taxation
1550 E. College Parkway, Suite 115
Carson City, NV 89706
(775) 687-4820
(800) 992-0900

New Hampshire
Department of Revenue Administration
45 Chenell Drive
P.O. Box 457
Concord, NH 03302-0457
(603) 271-2191
(603) 271-2186 Taxpayer Assistance

New Jersey
New Jersey Division of Taxation
Office of Information and Publications
P.O. Box 281
Trenton, NJ 08695-0281
(609) 292-6400

New Mexico
Department of Taxation and Revenue
1100 S. St. Francis Dr.
P.O. Box 630
Santa Fe, NM 87504-0630
(505) 827-0700

New York
NYS Tax Department

Taxpayer Assistance Bureau
W.A. Harriman Campus
Albany, NY 12227
(800) 225-5829

North Carolina
Secretary of State Corporations Division:
P.O. Box 29622
Raleigh, NC 27626-0622
(919) 807-2225

Department of Revenue:
P.O. Box 25000
Raleigh, N.C. 27640-0640
(919) 733-3991 General Information
(919) 733-4684 Taxpayer Assistance

North Dakota
State Tax Commission
600 E. Boulevard Ave.
Bismarck, ND 58505-0599
(701) 328-2770

Department of Taxation
1030 Freeway Drive North
Columbus, OH 43229
(800) 282-1780 Individual Income Taxpayer Services
(888) 405-4039 Business Taxpayer Assistance

Oklahoma
Tax Commission
2501 N. Lincoln Blvd.
Oklahoma City, OK 73194
(405) 521-4321

Oregon
Department of Revenue
Revenue Building

955 Center Street, N.E.
Salem, OR 97310-2555
(503) 378-4988
(800) 356-4222

Pennsylvania
Department of Revenue
11 Strawberry Square
Harrisburg, PA 17128-0101
(717) 787-1064

Rhode Island
Department of Administration
Division of Taxation
One Capital Hill
Providence, RI 02908-5800
(401) 222-1040

South Carolina
Department of Revenue
Columbia Mills Building
301 Gervais St., P.O. Box 125
Columbia, SC 29214
(800) 763-1295

South Dakota
Department of Revenue
445 E. Capital Ave.
Pierre, SD 57501-3185
(800) 829-9188

Tennessee
Department of Revenue
Andrew Jackson State Office Building
500 Deaderick St.
Nashville, TN 37242
(615) 253-0600
(800) 342-1003

Texas
State Comptroller
Taxpayer Assistance
LBJ State Office Building
111 E. 17th St.
Austin, TX 78774
(512) 463-4600
(888) 434-5464

Utah
Utah State Tax Commission
210 N. 1950 West
Salt Lake City, UT 84134
(801) 297-2200
(800) 662-4335

Vermont
Department of Taxes
Pavillion Office Building
109 State Street
Montpelier, VT 05609-1401
(802) 828-2551 Business Taxes
(802) 828-2865 Individual income and property programs

Virginia
Department of Taxation
Office of Customer Services
P.O. Box 1115
Richmond, VA 23218-1115
(804) 367-8031 Individual income tax
(804) 367-8037 Business tax

Washington
Washington State Department of Revenue
P.O. Box 47450
Olympia, WA 98504-7450
(800) 647-7706

West Virginia
Department of Revenue
Taxpayer Services Division
P.O. Box 3784
Charleston, WV 25337-3784
(304) 558-3333
(800) 982-8297

Wisconsin
Department of Revenue
2135 Rimrock Rd.
Madison, WI 53708-8933
(608) 266-2772

Wyoming
Department of Revenue and Taxation
122 W. 25th St.
Cheyenne, WY 82002-0110
(307) 777-7961

Appendix B

New Business Checklist

1. YOU MUST FIRST prepare a WBITTEN business plan and financial statements. Consult your financial advisors (accountant, lawyer, etc.) before undertaking these, and have the plan and statement reviewed by your advisors after completion.

2. Did you COMPLETE STEP 1? You must learn how very essential a business plan is for the success of your business.

3. Decide if your company will operate as a corporation, a partnership, a sole proprietorship or a non-profit organization.

4. Obtain incorporation papers from the Secretary of State. If your business is already incorporated in another state, contact the Secretary of State to get the proper application to do business in the new state.

5. Apply for a Federal Employer Identification Number (EIN) by filling out the Form SS-4. You may also call the local IRS hotline service, or visit the IRS's Web site: www.irs.gov.

6. Apply for a State Sales Tax Number if you plan to sell a taxable product or service.

7. Contact your state's Department of Labor or Employment for unemployment insurance registration materials.

8. Contact the Workers Compensation Commission to determine what's required for compliance with the Workers Compensation Act (this is not necessary for a sole proprietorship without employees).

9. Contact the local municipal office (town clerk, county clerk, etc.) to find out if there are any local registration or license requirements.

10. If you plan to operate your business from your home, check with the local code enforcement office to ensure compliance with all local requirements.

11. Contact the Bureau of Labor Standards office to find out what is necessary for compliance with the Occupational Safety and Health Act (OSHA).

12. Contact your state's Department of Taxation/Revenue to request the proper paperwork for registration, and to receive instructions on withholding and paying state income taxes, sales tax, excise tax, etc.

APPENDIX C

Entrepreneur Self-Test

The Entrepreneur Self-Test was developed by the Chamber of Commerce of West Alabama to be used as a resource. This is not a comprehensive or exact evaluation but can provide you with an overall view of your entrepreneurial potential. This test assesses your character qualities, problem-solving methods, motivations, relational skills, business knowledge and support system known to be critical in successful entrepreneurship.

Entrepreneur Self-Test

Yes	No		
		1	Would others describe you as persistent?
		2	Do you stay on task?
		3	Do you remain optimistic even in unpleasant situations?
		4	Are you self motivated?
		5	Are you innovative in finding solutions to problems and challenges?
		6	Do you mind working hard if that is what it takes to complete the task?
		7	Are you willing to make sacrifices to possibly gain lasting rewards?
		8	Are you willing to work long, demanding hours?
		9	Do you enjoy competition?
		10	Do you have an innovative idea that you see a significant need for?
		11	Can you make up your mind in a hurry if necessary?

12	Are you willing to take chances?
13	Are you adaptable to change?
14	Do you recover from set backs by taking a different approach and trying again?
15	Do you relate well to people on different levels?
16	Do you get along well with others?
17	Can you lead and inspire others?
18	Do you take full responsibility for consequences?
19	Have you ever worked as a manager or supervisor?
20	Would your family and friends be supportive of your new venture?
21	Do you regularly network with others to gain information and guidance?
22	Do you have the emotional strength to withstand the stress?
23	Do you have sound financial knowledge of how a business operates?
24	Do you understand the basics of the balance sheet and income statement?
25	Can you effectively keep accurate notes and records?

If you have been able to answer "yes" to 18 of the above questions then you have the potential to successfully start your own business.

If you answered "yes" to less than 18 questions then look for supplemental help in the areas you answered "no" to, by improving your own skills, hiring help or finding a business partner skilled in that area.

It takes a variety of different skills to successfully run a business, so look at each question to which you answered "no" as an opportunity for improvement.

APPENDIX D

Business Glossary of Terms

ACCOUNTING PERIOD

A regular period of time, such as a quarter or year, for which a financial statement is produced.

AFFIRMATIVE ACTION

Measures taken to correct the effects of past discrimination in hiring and promotion.

AGE DISCRIMINATION IN EMPLOYMENT ACT (ADEA)

Prohibits discrimination against individuals who are aged 40 or above.

AMERICANS WITH DISABILITIES ACT

Prohibits discrimination against persons with disabilities.

ARBITRATION

Means of settling a dispute between two parties in which the matter is decided by a third party chosen by the two disputants.

ASSET

Anything that can generate cash. Examples include accounts receivable (money customers owe you), inventory (stock or merchandise), equipment (furniture, fixtures, machinery, delivery trucks), and anything else that can generate cash.

AUDIT

Inspection and verification of financial accounts, records and accounting procedures.

BACKSOURCING

The expiration or termination of an outsourcing arrangement and the recapture in-house of the outsourced function.

BALANCE SHEET

Financial statement showing assets on the left side and liabilities on the right. A balance sheet provides an overview of a company's financial position at the given time.

BARTER

Trade in which merchandise is exchanged directly for other merchandise without the use of money. Barter is an important means of trade with countries using currency that is not readily convertible.

BEGINNING BALANCE SHEET

Financial snapshot of a business at the beginning of a period. It lists business's assets, liabilities, and owners' or stockholders' equity.

BENCHMARKING

A method of comparing contract services, prices, products, etc. to industry norms or best practice or other independent standards.

BILL OF LADING

Receipt given by a carrier to the shipper of goods.

BOILERPLATE

Standardized "fine-print" text in a contract or other agreement detailing terms and conditions.

BREAK-EVEN POINT

Volume of sales at which total costs equal total revenues. Sales above this volume generate profits.

BUSINESS DEVELOPMENT CORPORATION (BDC)

A business financing agency, usually made up of the financial institutions in an area or state, and organized for assisting in the financing of industrial concerns which are not able to obtain such assistance through normal channels. The "risk" is spread among various members of the BDC and interest rates may vary somewhat from those charged by member institutions.

BUSINESS OBJECTIVES

Can refer to any business operation, including product design, marketing, sales, finance, accounting, manufacturing, logistics, supply chain management, customer relationship management and other special business relationships.

BUSINESS PLAN

A blueprint and communication tool for your business. A device to help you, the owner, set out how you intend to operate your business. A road map to tell others how you expect to get there.

BUSINESS PROCESS

Means a sequence of defined steps necessary to achieve a business objective.

BUSINESS PROCESS OUTSOURCING (BPO)

Is the procurement of particular services that involve ongoing outsourcing of specific business processes.

C&F

"Cost and Freight"—commercial term meaning that the stated value of a shipment of goods includes all costs and freight involved in shipping the goods to their destination.

CAPACITY

The ability to repay a debt.

CAPITAL

Money available to invest or the total of accumulated assets available for production.

CASH FLOW

The actual movement of cash. Used to measure cash inflow minus cash outflow.

CASH FLOW PROJECTION

A forecast of the cash (checks or money orders) a business anticipates receiving and disbursing during the course of a given span of time—frequently a month. It is useful in anticipating the cash portion of your business at specific times during the period projected.

CASH PLAN

Shows you how much cash is coming into the business and how much cash is going out. It also shows how much cash will be left over or how much additional cash will be needed to pay for expenses.

CERTIFIED LENDERS

Banks that participate in the SBA's guaranteed loan program, have a good track record with the SBA and agree to certain conditions set forth by the SBA. In return, the SBA agrees to process any guaranteed loan application within three business days. District offices of the SBA can provide lists of certified banks in their areas.

CIVIL RIGHTS ACT OF 1966

Prohibits discrimination based on race or ethnic origin.

COLA

"Cost of Living Adjustment"—periodic changes in wages or benefits designed to compensate for the effects of inflation.

COLLATERAL

Property, stocks, bonds, savings accounts, life insurance and current business assets—any or all of which may be held or assumed to insure repayment of a loan.

COMMODITY

Any good exchanged in trade. Usually refers to raw materials and agricultural products traded principally on the basis of price.

COMPETITION

Rivalry. Similar businesses providing products or services to your potential customers.

COMPETITIVE INSOURCING

Involves a process where internal employees may engage in bidding to compete with competitive, third-party bidders for a defined scope of work.

COMPOUND INTEREST

Interest earned on previously accumulated interest as well as the principle.

CONFERENCE CALL

Telephone call among three or more people in different locations.

CO-SOURCING

Is a term used by one external services provider to trademark its brand of outsourcing services.

COTTAGE INDUSTRY

Business or industry in which goods are produced primarily in the home of the producer.

CREDIT BUREAU

Company that compiles and maintains information on consumer credit and provides the information to potential creditors for a fee.

CREDIT RATING

Evaluation of an individual's or corporation's history of repaying past loans. Credit ratings are used as a benchmark to assess the future ability of a creditor to pay back loans.

CROSS PROMOTIONS

Promoting with other company's products.

CURRENT RATIO

Current Assets/Current Liabilities. This ratio should be 1.0 or greater for liquidity. If it drops below 1.0, the ability to pay bills is impaired. If it is greater than 1.0, there is a possibility that assets are not being used efficiently to generate new revenue.

CUSTOMER RELATIONSHIP MANAGEMENT (CRM)

A marketing and fulfillment system that usually includes a call center, databases, software and marketing strategy.

DEBT-TO-EQUITY

Total Debt/Total Owner's Investment. Measures how much of the company's assets have been acquired by debt versus by owner's funds. If the ratio is greater than 1.0, it means more of the money came from outside sources. Need to closely monitor sales level to ensure your ability to service outside debt.

DEMOGRAPHICS

The statistics of an area's population. This includes characteristics of the population that influence consumption of products and services. They include age, sex, race, family size, level of education, occupation, income and location of residence.

DEPRECIATION

Decrease in the value of equipment from wear and tear and the passage of time. Depreciation on business equipment is generally deductible for tax purposes.

DESKTOP PUBLISHING

Creation of books and other written material using a desktop computer for word processing, graphics and layout.

DIRECT LOANS

Financial assistance provided through the lending of federal monies for a specific period of time, with a reasonable expectation of repayment. Such loans may or may not require the payment of interest.

DIRECT MARKETING

Sales and promotion technique in which the promotional materials are delivered individually to potential customers via direct mail, telemarketing, door-to-door selling or other direct means.

EMPLOYER IDENTIFICATION NUMBER (EIN)

A number obtained by a business from the IRS by filing application form SS-4. The number is to be shown on all business tax returns, documents and statements. Wholesalers often request this number in order to offer wholesale prices to retailers.

ENTREPRENEUR

Innovator. One who recognizes opportunities and organizes resources to take advantage of the opportunity.

EQUAL EMPLOYMENT OPPORTUNITY ACT

Prohibits discrimination. Any employee or applicant for employment who believes that they have been discriminated against because of their race, color, religion, sex, national origin, sexual orientation, age, physical or mental disability, and/or reprisal in an employment matter may file a complaint of discrimination.

EQUAL PAY ACT OF 1963

Prohibits employers from paying different wages to men and women who perform essentially the same work under similar working conditions.

EQUITY

Is calculated by subtracting your liabilities from your assets. Equity shows how much a business has, how much it owes, and the difference is the equity level.

ESCROW

Temporary deposit with a third party of assets by agreement between two parties to a contract. The money is released when the conditions of the contract have been met.

EXPENSE ACCOUNT

Account often used by salespersons or executives for travel and entertainment expenses.

FEASIBILITY STUDY

Likelihood study. A way to determine if a business idea is capable of being achieved. (Asks the question, "Can it work and produce the level of profit necessary?")

FEATURES

Characteristics of a product or service.

FEATURES/BENEFITS

Approach to promoting based on the understanding that a product's FEATURES are of little importance to the customer unless they are a source of BENEFIT to the customer.

FIDUCIARY

Person or company entrusted with assets owned by another party (beneficiary), and is responsible for investing the assets until they are turned over to the beneficiary.

FINANCIALS

Documents that record the monetary standing of a company. They include but are not limited to: balance sheet, profit and loss projections, cash plans, and ratio analysis reports.

FINANCIAL HISTORY (PERSONAL)

This is a picture of your personal financial condition to date. It is a very important part of any loan application and/or interview, especially when a loan for a projected new business is under consideration. A complete Personal Financial History is a record of borrowing and repayments; an itemized listing of your personal assets and liabilities.

FISCAL YEAR

Any 12-month period used by a company or government as an accounting period.

FIXED COST

Any cost of production which does not vary significantly with the volume of output.

FIXED EXPENSE

Any costs not related directly to the production of your product or service. Indirect costs include such things as rent, insurance, and basic utilities.

FLEXTIME

Work schedule in which the worker is required only to work a minimum number of hours, and is given latitude in deciding when to report for and leave work.

FREE ON BOARD

Commercial term under which the seller's obligations are fulfilled when the goods reach a point specified in the contract. For example, "F.O.B., Seller's Warehouse" means that the buyer assumes all costs and risks once the goods reach the seller's warehouse.

FULFILLMENT

Process of receiving orders and shipping and tracking goods sold through direct marketing.

GROSS MARGIN

Gross Profit/Total Sales. The percentage of every dollar earned that can be used to pay general and administrative expenses.

GRACE PERIOD

Time allowed a debtor in which legal action will not be undertaken by the creditor when payment is late.

GROSS PROFIT

Sales minus Cost of Goods Sold. The total dollars available to cover general and administrative expenses such as utilities, advertising, rent, etc.

GUARANTEED/INSURED LOANS

Programs in which the federal government makes an arrangement to indemnify a lender against part or all of any defaults by those responsible for repayment of loans.

HARD COPY

Printout of information stored on a computer.

IMMIGRATION REFORM AND CONTROL ACT OF 1986

Prohibits discrimination on the basis of national origin or citizenship of persons who are authorized to work in the United States.

INCOME & EXPENSES

Accounting motion picture. The inflow versus outflow of money.

INCUBATORS

Incubators encourage entrepreneurship and minimize obstacles to new business formation and growth, particularly for high technology firms, by housing in one facility a number of fledgling enterprises which share an array of services. These shared services may include: meeting areas, secretarial services, accounting, research library, on-site professional and management counseling, and computer word processing facilities.

INDEMNIFICATION

Is a method of shifting legal liability from one party to another by contract.

INDEMNITY

Obligation of one party to reimburse another party for losses which have occurred or which may occur.

INDICIA

Preprinted marking on each piece of a bulk mailing which shows that postage has been paid by the sender.

INSOURCING

Is the transfer of an outsourced function to an internal department of the customer, to be managed entirely by employees.

INTRAPRENEUR

A person within a large corporation who takes direct responsibility for turning an idea into a profitable finished product through assertive risk-taking and innovation. An intrapreneur is an entrepreneur within a large firm.

INTRAPRENEURSHIP

Fostering entrepreneurism within established organizations.

JOB SHARING

Arrangement in which the responsibilities and hours of one job position are carried out by two people.

LEAD TIME

Period of time required to prepare for a certain stage of a project. For example, the lead time in introducing a new product is the time it takes for research, development, market research, and factory preparation.

LETTER OF CREDIT (L/C)

May be revocable or irrevocable—A document, consisting of specific instructions by a buyer of goods, that is issued by a bank to the seller who is authorized to draw a specified sum of money under certain conditions, i.e., the receipt by the bank of certain documents within a given time. An irrevocable L/C provides a guarantee by the issuing bank in the event that all terms and conditions are met by the buyer (or drawee). A revocable L/C can be canceled or altered by the drawee after it has been issued by drawee's bank. A confirmed L/C is one issued by a foreign bank which is validated or guaranteed by a U.S. bank for a U.S. exporter in the case of default by the foreign buyer or bank.

LIABILITIES

Includes accounts payable (money you owe to suppliers), plus all current costs of doing business (mortgage payments, insurance, taxes, salaries, utilities).

LIABILITY

Is the legal obligation arising out of a failure to honor one's legal liability to another party, such as by contract or in tort.

LIEN

Legal right to hold property of another party or to have it sold or applied in payment of a claim.

LIQUIDATION

Sale of the assets of a business (e.g. to pay off debts).

LIST PRICE

Price at which manufacturers recommend retailers sell a good. The list price is often reduced at the point of sale by the retailer to promote sales.

LOCAL DEVELOPMENT CORPORATION

An organization, usually made up of local citizens, designed to improve the economy of the area by including business and industry to locate there. A local development corporation usually has financing capabilities.

LOSS LEADER Merchandise sold by a retailer at a loss in order to increase store traffic and sales of other items.

MARGINAL COST

Additional cost associated with producing one more units of output.

MARKET RESEARCH INFORMATION

An orderly, objective way of learning about the people who will buy your product or use your service.

MARKET SEGMENTATION

Division of the market or population into sub-groups with similar motivations. Widely used bases for segmenting include geographic differences, personality differences, demographic differences, use-of-product differences, and psychographic differences.

MARKETING

The process of planning and executing the conception, pricing, promotion and distribution of ideas, goods, and services to create exchanges that satisfy individual and organizational objectives.

MASSIVE OUTSOURCING

Refers to the process where a majority of the business support processes are outsourced in one transaction or a small number of related transactions.

MINORITY BUSINESSES

The Small Business Administration defines minorities as those who are "socially or economically disadvantaged". The regulations set forth the specific criteria. Social disadvantage has to do with membership of one of several different racial or ethnic categories as defined by regulation, or on a case-by-case basis for others who feel they are socially disadvantaged. Groups which are considered to be socially disadvantaged include: Black Americans; Hispanic Americans; Native Americans (American Indians, Eskimos, Aleuts, or Native Hawaiians); Asian Pacific Americans (persons with origins from Japan, China, the Philippines, Vietnam, Korea, Samoa, Guam, U.S. Trust Territory of the Pacific Islands, Northern Mariana Islands, Laos, Cambodia or Taiwan); and Subcontinent Asian Americans. Economic disadvantage has to do with the barriers that social disadvantage has placed in the way of an individual's participation in education, business, employment etc. SBA district offices have minority business specialists who can help with the definitions. In most cases, being a woman does not by itself qualify as minority status.

NETWORKING

Using contacts made in business for purposes beyond the reason for the initial contact. For example, a sales representative may ask a customer for names of others who may be interested in his product.

OFFICE OF SMALL AND DISADVANTAGED BUSINESS UTILIZATION

Each agency of the federal government with significant procurement authority has an office that is responsible for assuring that the agency complies with federal regulations to purchase a certain percentage of products and services from small and minority-owned and operated businesses. Small businesses with procurement problems or questions are advised to first contact a procurement center representative, a GSA business service center, or agency contracting officers. If the small firm cannot receive help, however, it can contact the OSDBU in Washington.

OUTSOURCE

To obtain components for a product from sources outside the company

OUTSOURCING (OR SOURCING)

Is the transfer (or delegation) to an external service provider of the operation and day-to-day management of a business process.

OVERHEAD

Business expenses not directly related to a particular good or service produced. Examples are insurance, utilities, and rent.

PREFERRED LENDERS

Banks which have a special written agreement with the SBA which allows them to make a guaranteed SBA loan without prior SBA approval. Preferred loans have a maximum SBA guarantee of 80 percent. Call SBA district offices for more information.

PRIMARY RESEARCH

Information collected by interview or questionnaire designed for a specific need.

PROCUREMENT ASSISTANCE

Procurement can be a good source of income for small business owners if the business has a product or service of interest to federal agencies. Small businesses should be particularly interested in two types of procurement: small business set-asides, which are procurement opportunities required for all contracts under $10,000 or a certain percentage of an agency's total procurement expenditure; and the SBA 8(a) program in which small businesses and minority-owned and operated businesses are admitted to the program and can tender on special contracts. Sources for procurement information include SBA district and regional offices, GSA Business Service Center, procurement center representatives of the SBA, and agency offices of Small and Disadvantaged Business Utilization (OSDBU). Many states have their own programs; check state program lists.

PROFIT SHARING

Compensation arrangement whereby employees receive additional pay or benefits when the company earns or increases profit.

PRO FORMA

A projection or estimate of what may result in the future from actions in the present. Estimate of how the business will turn out if certain assumptions are achieved.

PROFIT & LOSS STATEMENT

A detailed earnings statement for the previous full year (if you are currently in business). Existing businesses are required to show a Profit and Loss Statement for the current period to the date of the Balance Sheet.

PSYCHOGRAPHICS

Psychological profiles of potential customers in a market. Attitudes, interests, and opinions.

QUOTA

The quantity of goods of a specific kind that a country permits to be imported without restriction or imposition of additional duties.

RN NUMBER

Number assigned to clothing manufacturers for labeling garments. The RN number allows the manufacturer of a certain brand to be determined. Information on obtaining RN numbers is available from the Federal Trade Commission.

ROI

Return on investment

SCORE

The Service Corps of Retired Executives is a volunteer management assistance program of the SBA. SCORE volunteers provide one-on-one counseling and workshops and seminars for small firms. Those interested should contact SBA district offices for an application for counseling. SCORE chapters exist throughout the nation.

SEASONALITY

Changes in business, employment or buying patterns which occur predictably at given times of the year.

SECONDARY RESEARCH

Information already collected for general needs, such as census data. Readily available in published form.

SHELF LIFE

Length of time before a good spoils or becomes obsolete.

SIMPLE INTEREST

Interest paid only on the principal of a loan. No interest is paid on interest accrued during the term of the loan.

SOURCING

Is determining "who" will do "what" to fulfill enterprise responsibilities.

SPREADSHEET

Table of numerical data in which columns and rows are related by formulae.

STANDARD INDUSTRIAL CLASSIFICATION CODE (SIC CODE NUMBER)

A four digit number assigned to identify a business based on the type of business or trade and manufacturing, while the last two digits correspond to subgroups such as constructing homes versus constructing highways. A business can determine its SIC number by looking it up in a directory published by the Department of Commerce, or by checking in the SIC book in the reference section of a local library. SBA size standards are based on SIC codes.

SURETY BONDS

Surety bonds provide reimbursement to an individual, company or the government if a firm fails to complete a contract. SBA guarantees surety bonds in a program much like SBA's guaranteed loan program.

TAX NUMBER

A number assigned to a business by a state revenue department that enables the business to buy wholesale without paying sales tax on goods and products. Contact the state government's department of revenue.

TELEMARKETING

Use of the telephone to market goods or services directly to prospective customers and/or to receive orders and inquiries generated from other advertising and promotions.

TEST MARKET

Process of conducting a small-scale promotion or introduction of a good in order to gather information useful in a broader promotion or product introduction.

TITLE VII OF THE CIVIL RIGHTS ACT OF 1964

Prohibits discrimination on the basis of race, color, religion, national origin and sex. It also prohibits sex discrimination on the basis of pregnancy and sexual harassment.

VENTURE CAPITAL

Money used to support new or unusual undertakings; equity, risk or speculative investment capital. This funding is provided to new or existing firms which exhibit potential for above-average growth.

VESTING

Granting to employees entitlement to a pension at retirement.

VIRAL MARKETING

Viral marketing is the extremely powerful and unique ability of the Internet to build self-propagating visitor streams, bringing about exponential growth to a company's Web site. This can consist of such things as affiliate programs, co-branding, link exchanges, e-mail campaigns, and off-line promotion.

W-4 FORM

The form provides two critical pieces of information: the employee's Social Security Number and the allowances the employee is claiming for income tax withholding purposes.

WATS

"Wide Area Telephone Service"—special long-distance calling service offered by telecommunications companies which offer reduced-rate long distance calls for commercial users.

WAY BILL

Document which accompanies goods in shipment and which details the cost and route of shipment.

WORK PERMIT

Document given to resident aliens which demonstrates to employers that the individual is legally allowed to work in the United States.

ZIP CODE + 4

Nine digit code used on mail to identify very specifically the destination of the mailpiece.

APPENDIX E

Evaluating Start-Up Costs

When starting a new business, there will be start-up or one-time expenses. Use this chart to evaluate your financial needs and budget.

Evaluating Start-Up Costs

Item	Dollar Cost
Real Estate, furniture, fixtures, machinery, equipment:	
a) Purchase price—if paid in full with cash	$ _____
b) Cash down payment—if purchased on contract	$ _____
c) Transportation & installation costs	$ _____
Starting Inventory	$ _____
Decorating, refurbishment, & remodeling costs	$ _____
Deposits Required:	
a) Utilities	$ _____
b) Rent	$ _____
c) Other (identify)	$ _____
Fees Required:	
a) Legal, accounting, others	$ _____
b) Licenses, permits, etc.	$ _____
c) Other (identify)	$ _____
Initial Advertising & Marketing Costs (ie., flyers, sales letters and calls, signs, brochures, etc.)	$ _____

Accounts Receivable (_____ days of sales)	$ _____
Salaries and owners draw until business enterprise opens or until cash flow is positive	$ _____
Other miscellaneous expenses:	
Merchant Association fees, equipment rental, office supplies,	$ _____
cleaning service, other supplies, signs, etc.	$ _____
Payments on other fixed obligations	$ _____
Total Start-Up Costs	$ _____

(SCORE, Fort Worth, TX, 4/97)

Appendix F

Start-Up To-Do-List for Small Businesses

_____ 1.   Know what type of business you would like to start and learn all you can about it.

_____ 2.   Appraise your business strengths and weaknesses. Be strict and objective.

_____ 3.   Conduct thorough research of potential customers, your trade or industry, your competition, your licensing and tax requirements, location, and name.

_____ 4.   Determine type of business organization (ie. Proprietorship, Partnership, or Corporation)

_____ 5.   Evaluate possible site locations. Check physical condition, suitability, traffic flow, parking, utility requirements, and cost.

_____ 6.   Prepare a comprehensive business plan—include your action timetable.

_____ 7.   Decide on your business hours.

_____ 8.   Secure necessary capital. (Bank loan, budget to save, borrow on insurance, etc.)

_____ 9.   Obtain needed facilities, equipment, furnishings, signage, supplies, stock.

_____ 10.   Recruit personnel. Establish job descriptions and training program.

_____ 11.   Print business cards, stationery, invoice or statement forms.

_____ 12.   Register name of business (your assumed name) and/or file articles of incorporation with the Secretary of State. Publish notice in newspaper.

_____ 13.   Secure any necessary permits, licenses, or zoning variations. Check with both local and state licensing agencies.

_____ 14.   Register your business with the state and obtain a Sales & Use Tax Permit (if applicable).

_____ 15.   Register for Federal tax number (Form SS-4) and obtain employee tax and with holding information from the IRS.

_____ 16.   Establish bank account (separate from personal account). Shop for the bank and services that best suit your needs.

_____ 17.   If you intend to hire employees in your business, phone your Department of Economic Security or Workforce Commission.

_____ 18.   Phone the IRS for a free "Small Business Tax Kit" at 1-800-829-3676. For information about free Tax Education Workshops, call 1-800-829-1040 or check out the IRS website for this information.

_____ 19.   Issue news releases. Publicize your new venture.

(Women in New Development, Bemidji, MN, 4/97)

APPENDIX G

Stats for Minority Business Owners

Self-employment as a share of the labor group is 3.8 percent for African Americans; 6.4 percent American Indian, Eskimo or Aleut; and 10.1 percent Asian or Pacific Islander.

Of U.S. businesses, 5.8 percent are owned by Hispanic Americans, 4.4 percent by Asian Americans, 4.0 percent for African Americans and 0.9 percent by American Indians.

Of minority-owned businesses, 39.5 percent are Hispanic-owned, 30.0 percent Asian-owned, 27.1 percent African American-owned and 6.5 percent American Indian-owned.

Of the 4,514,699 jobs in minority-owned businesses in 1997, 48.8 percent were in Asian-owned firms, 30.8 percent in Hispanic-owned firms, 15.9 percent in African American-owned firms and 6.6 percent in American Native-owned firms.

Minority-owned firms had about $96 billion in payroll in 1997.

The minority-owned business share of U.S. firms was 6.8 percent in 1982; it grew steadily to 9.3 percent in 1987; 12.5 percent in 1992; and 14.6 percent in 1997.

In 1997, there were 823,500 black-owned businesses in the U.S. employing 718,300 people and generating $71.2 billion in revenues.

Almost 4 in 10 black-owned businesses (38 percent) were owned by women.

47 percent of all black-owned firms were in six states: New York, California, Texas, Florida, Georgia and Maryland.

Hispanic-owned businesses in the U.S. totaled 1.2 million firms in 1997, employed over 1 million people and generated nearly $200 billion in revenue. Just under 4 in 10 of these firms were owned by people of Mexican origin.

73 percent of Hispanic-owned businesses were in four states; New York, California, Texas and Florida.

In 1997, there were 197,300 American Indian- and Alaska Native-owned businesses in the United States, employing 298,700 people and generating $34.3 billion in revenues. These businesses made up 0.9 percent of the 20.8 million non-farm businesses in the nation and generated 0.2 percent of their receipts.

Asian-and Pacific Islander (API)-owned businesses in the U.S. totaled about 913,000 in 1997, employed more than 2.2 million people and generated $306.9 billion in revenues.

Since 1997, the number of Native American-owned businesses has jumped by 84 percent to 197,300. Eighty-five percent of these firms can be described as micro-enterprises.

In 2000, 10.7 percent or 28.1 million people in the United States spoke Spanish at home, and 49 percent of them spoke English less than "very well."

(Source: U.S. Small Business Administration Office of Advocacy, U.S. Census Bureau and the Corporation for Enterprise Development.)

APPENDIX H

Stats for Women Business Owners

According to the Center for Women's Business Research, currently one in 18 (6%) U.S. women are business owners.

There were over 6 million women-owned businesses in 2002. Women of color owned 1.2 million of these firms.

Women-owned firms represent 28% of all U.S. businesses, generating $1.15 trillion in sales, and 20% of these firms are owned by women of color. In other words, one in five wo men-owned firms is owned by a woman of color.

Between 1997 and 2002, the number of women-owned firms increased by 14% nationwide, twice the rate of all firms (14% vs. 7%). Firms owned by women of color increased by 32%.

From 1997 to 2002, the greatest growth in the number of women-owned firms was in "non-traditional" industries including construction, agricultural services, transportation/communications, and finance/insurance/real estate.

Women-owned businesses are just as financially strong and creditworthy as the average U.S. firm, with similar performance on bill payment and similar levels of credit risk.

Women business owners are more likely than male business owners to use the Internet for business—61% of women compared to 55% of men. Among Internet users, women and men business owners are equally likely to have Web sites (50% to 54% respectively).

The workforce of women-owned firms shows more gender equity. Women business owners overall employ a roughly gender-balanced workforce (52% women and 48% men), while male business owners employ, on average, 38% women and 62% men.

Women-owned firms in the. U.S. are more likely than all firms to offer flex-time, tuition reimbursement, and profit, sharing to their employees.

Women business owners are philanthropically active: seven in 10 volunteer at least once per month; 31% contribute $5,000 or more to charity annually; 15% give $10,000 or more. Women are also more likely to serve in volunteer leadership positions than men.

Women business owners cite frustration with work environment, the desire for greater challenges, and more flexibility as motives for becoming entrepreneurs

Appendix I

Myths Regarding Entrepreneurs

Myth 1:   **Entrepreneurs are born, not made**
Some entrepreneurs are born with the talent for innovation, energy, attributes; however, they need more: work experience, know-how, a network of contacts, business skills; and other attributes that can be acquired with proper coaching.

Myth 2:   **Anyone can start a business; it is about luck and bravery**
Some entrepreneurs need to see the difference between idea and opportunity; need to act like an entrepreneur.

Myth 3:   **Entrepreneurs are gamblers**
Entrepreneurs take calculated risks; they fry to influence the odds by getting others to share risks; they won't shy away from necessary risk.

Myth 4:   **Entrepreneurs want to run the show**
If you try to do everything yourself, it will limit your growth.

Myth 5:   **Entrepreneurs are their own bosses and completely independent**
Successful entrepreneurs have a network of partners, investors, customers, employers, supplies they rely on.

Myth 6:   **Entrepreneurs work longer and harder than managers in corporate**
Some entrepreneurs may work longer hours and some do not. Both jobs are demanding.

Myth 7:   **Entrepreneurs have greater stress, pressure & pay a higher personal price**
There is no evidence that entrepreneurs are more stressed; however, there could be a sense of accomplishment, fun and flexibility

Myth 8:   Starting a business is risky and often ends in failure
This is true in many cases; 80% fail in the first 5 years; but success is higher for higher-potential ventures with experienced talented people who attract right people and finances.

Myth 9:   New business start-up is for the young and energetic
Being young and energetic may help, but age is no barrier; age brings experience and financial stability

Myth 10:   Money is the most important part of success
If the other important parts are there money tends to follow

Myth 11:   Entrepreneurs are motivated by a quest for money
Growth minded more motivated by challenge to build rather than instant money; money can be viewed as a tool to keep score

Myth 12:   Entrepreneurs seek power, control over others to feel in charge
Successful entrepreneurs strive for responsibility, achievement and results rather than power. They thrive on accomplishment and outperforming the competition. Control comes from the results they achieve.

Appendix J

Women vs Men

More than half of women business owners (53 percent) emphasize intuition or "right-brain" instead of "left-brain," which emphasizes analysis, the processing of information methodically, and developing procedures. Intuitive processes often allow someone to see opportunities that aren't readily apparent and to know if they are right without the use of reason and analysis.

The way in which women business owners make decisions is usually more whole-brained than men's (i.e. it is more evenly distributed between right-brain and left-brain). This allows someone to use creative and analytical processes, a characteristic that, is critical for small business management, especially in uncertain situations.

Women business owners tend to reflect on decisions, and to weigh options and outcomes before taking action. In addition, women don't hesitate to gather information from business advisors and associates. The advantage here is the shared knowledge that is gathered through interpersonal interactions and liaisons.

Women entrepreneurs describe their businesses m family terms and see then business relationships as a network. This "personal touch" is often what drives employee motivation and productivity. The downside is however that they may lack policies and procedures which are clearly stated.

Women have the ability to balance different tasks and priorities. In business for themselves or for someone else, the ability to be flexible and adaptable is a distinct advantage these days when everyone is expected to perform many duties.

Women entrepreneurs rend to find satisfaction and Success from building relationships with customers and employees, from having control of then own destiny, and from doing something that they consider worthwhile. We spend the majority of our lives at work. If our work and our personal values are not in alignment, sooner or later we feel conflict. Women entrepreneurs have used this internal conflict as a motivation in order to create, the life that they desire.

Entrepreneurs in general are more similar to each other than they are to the working population in general. Compared to the general working population, entrepreneurs tend to be more logical and analytical in the way they make decisions, no matter their sex.

(American Women's Economic Development Corporation, Stamford, CT; based on information gathered by the National Foundation for Women Business Owners, 4/97)

APPENDIX K

10 Characteristics of Successful Entrepreneurs

1. **An eye for opportunity:** Many entrepreneurs start by finding a need and quickly satisfying it.

2. **Independence:** Even though most entrepreneurs know how to work within the framework for the sake of profits, they enjoy being their own boss.

3. **An appetite for hard work:** Most entrepreneurs start out working long, hard hours with little pay.

4. **Self-confidence:** Entrepreneurs must demonstrate extreme self-confidence in order to cope with all the risks of operating their own business.

5. **Discipline:** Successful entrepreneurs resist the temptation to do what is unimportant or the easiest but have the ability to think through to what is the most essential.

6. **Judgment:** Successful entrepreneurs have, the ability to think quickly and make a wise decision.

7. **Ability to accept change:** Change occurs frequently when you own your own business, the entrepreneur thrives on changes and their businesses grow.

8. **Make stress work for them:** On the roller coaster to business success the entrepreneur often copes by focusing on the end result and not the process of getting there.

9. **Need to achieve:** Although they keep an "eye" on profits, this is often secondary to the drive toward personal success.

10. **Focus on profits:** Successful entrepreneurs always have the profit margin in sight and know that their business success is measured by profits.

References

Advani, Asheesh. "Should You Turn Your Hobby Into a Business?: 5 Questions to Answer Before You Make the Leap from Hobbyist to Full-Time Entrepreneur." *Entrepreneur Magazine*, May (1994): 1-2.

Allers, Kimberly L. "The New Black Power on Wall Street." *Fortune* 149, No. 13 June (2004): 126-8, 130, 132, 134.

Belker, L. B. *First Time Manager.* American Management Association.

Bennett-Alexander, D and L. Hartman. *Employment Law for Business.* New York: Irwin McGraw-Hill, 2001.

Bennis, Warren. Learning *to Lead: A Workbook on Becoming a Leader.* Perseus Books/Addison Wesley, 1997.

Blanchard, Kenneth and Norman Peale. *The Power of Ethical Management: Why the Ethical Way Is the Profitable Way, in Your Life & in Your Business.* New York: William Morrow & Company, Inc., 1988.

Bradley, Anthony B. *The Rise of the Black Entrepreneur: A new force for economic and moral leadership.* Acton Institute http://www.acton.org/ppolicy/comment/article.php?id=137.

Breeding, C. "Emotional Intelligence Integral to Success." *The Business Journal,* December 10, 1999.

Choi, Yung Rok and Shepard, Dean A. 'Entrepreneurs' Decisions to Exploit Opportunities." *Journal of Management* 30 No. 3 (2004): 377-395.

Cohen, Neil. "The Five Ages of the Entrepreneur." *Venture Magazine,* July (1980): 40-42.

Conlin, Michelle. "The Rise of the Mompreneurs." *Business Week* No. 3886 June (2004): 70, 72.

Caceras, Maria. "Success is a Marathon: Entrepreneurs Find Success on Their Own Terms," *The Miami Herald*, August 8, 2004.

Dunn, M. "What is outsourcing?" Credits and Collections, http://www.credit-and-collections.com/article-misc-outsourcing.html.

Enbar, N. "Can 'Entrepreneurship' Become a Buzzword?" *Frontier Magazine*. February 9, 1999.

Enbar, N. "For an Entrepreneurial Edge, Go to B-School?" *Frontier Magazine*. April 16, 1999.

Enbar, N. "You Don't Need an MBA to Network on the Net" *Frontier Magazine*. January 25, 1999.

Fossum, J. *Labor Relations: Development, Structure, Process*. New York: McGraw-Hill Higher Education, 2002.

Gabriel, G. "What is Emotional Intelligence?" The Brain Connection. http://www.brainconnection.com/topics/?main=fa/emotional-intelligence. May 2000.

Gardner, H.. *Multiple Intelligences: The Theory in Practice*. NewYork: Basic Books, 1993.

Gartner, W. B. "Who is an Entrepreneur?" is the wrong question. *American Journal of Small Business,* 13 (Spring 1988): 11-32.

Gatewood, E. J., Pieterman, M. A., & Shaver, K. G. *Expectations and Entrepreneurial Persistence*. Paper presented at the Babson Entrepreneurship Research Conference, Houston, (1993).

Gatewood, R and H. Field. *Human Resource Selection*. Florida: Harcourt, Inc. 2001.

Goleman, D. *Destructive Emotions: How We Can Overcome Them*. New York: Bantam, 2003

Goleman, D. *Emotional Intelligence: Why it can matter more than IQ*. New York: Bantam, 1995.

Goleman, D. "Leadership That Gets Results." *Harvard Business Review*, March-April 2000.

Goleman, D. "What Makes a Leader." *Harvard Business Review*, Nov-Dec. 1998.

Goleman, D. *Working With Emotional Intelligence*. New York: Bantam, 1998.

Goleman, D., Boyatzis, R. & McKee, A. *Primal Leadership: Realizing the Power of Emotional Intelligence*. Boston: Harvard Business Press, 2002

"Habit Your Way" *Entrepreneur* 32 no. 3 March (2004): 94-95.

Hatten, T. S. *Small Business: Entrepreneurship and Beyond*. New Jersey: Prentice-Hall, 1997.

Henricks, Mark. What Not to Do. *Entrepreneur Magazine*. February (2004): 1-5.

Knox, Tim W. "Procurement Help from the SBA.: *Entrepreneur Magazine*. March (2004): 1-2.

Kurlantzick, Joshua. "About Face: The face of entrepreneurship has evolved over the years, and today, it's dramatically different. But what will the entrepreneur of the future look like?" *Entrepreneur Magazine*, January (2004): 1-3.

Mabrey, Wendy. "Should You Start Your Own Business?" *Women in Business* 56 No. 3 May/June (2004): 16-18.

Mancuso, J. R. "Are You Qualified to be an Entrepreneur?" *Wall Street Journal* November 23, 2003, final edition.

Mangan, Katherine S. "Entrepreneurs in Every Department." *The Chronicle of Higher Education* 50 No. 38 May (2004): A10-11.

McCarthy, E. "Entrepreneurial Students More Grounded." *Washington Post*, March 19, 2002. Page E05.

McGrath, R. G. *The Entrepreneurial Mindset*. Boston, Massachusetts: Harvard Business School Press, 2000.

McGregor, D. *The Human Side of Enterprise*. New York: McGraw-Hill, 1960.

Mello, J.A. *Strategic Human Resource Management.* Ohio: Southwestern, Thompson Learning. 2002.

Mercer, I. "The Brain Drain is Also Exodus of Entrepreneurial Talent." *The Calgary Herald*, February 2003.

Milkovich, G and J. Newman. *Compensation.* New York: Mc-Graw Hill Higher Education. 2002.

Moran, Gwen. "Now They Know: Getting word of your business out on the street is worth any price, but with these 7 marketing techniques, it's actually pretty cheap." *Entrepreneur's Be Your Own Boss Magazine,* January (2003): 1-4.

Moran, Gwen. "Promoting for Pennies: Marketing costs weighing you down? Here are 20 creative ways to boost business without breaking the bank." *Entrepreneur's Be Your Own Boss Magazine,* February (2004): 1-2.

Naffziger, D. W., Hornsby, J. S & Kuratko, D. F. A Proposed Research Model of Entrepreneurial Motivation. *Entrepreneurship Theory & Practice* 18 No.3 (1994)

National Commission on Entrepreneurship. *Five Myths About Entrepreneurs: Understanding How Businesses Start and Grow.* March 2001.

National Association of Women Business Owners and Online Women's Business Center, St. Louis, MO, May 1997.

National Women's Business Center, Washington, D.C., July 1997.

Neilson, A. "Are You the Entrepreneurial Type?" *Entrepreneur Magazine*, August 2002.

Newton, D. and M. Hendricks. "Can Entrepreneurship be Taught?" *Entrepreneur Magazine*, April 2003.

Nolle, T. "Beware the Pitfalls of Outsourcing" *Network Magazine*, September 2000.

Norcross, J. "Avoiding the Five Pitfalls." *Darwin Magazine*, April 2004.

Ohio Women's Business Resource Network, Columbus, OH, April 1997.

Pfeffer, J. *Power in Organizations.* Massachussets: Pitman Publishing, 1981.

Ramachandran, Nisha. "Be Your Own Boss." *U.S. News & World Report* 137 No. 3 August (2004): 62-63 and 65-66.

Robbins, Stever. "How Do I Start a Business?" *Entrepreneur Magazine.* February (2004): 1-3.

Rosenberg, H. "This Generation Is All Business." *Business Week Enterprise.* March 1, 1999.

Sandbulte, A. "Lead Don't Manage." *Industry Week* 242 No. 21. November 1, 1993: 16-18.

Schein, E. H. *Organizational Culture and Leadership.* San Francisco: Jossey-Bass, 1992.

Schein, E.H.. "Entrepreneurs: What they're really like." *Vocational Education Journal* 64 No. 80 (1994): 42-44.

Shaver, K.. G., Williams, S. L., & Scott, L. R. *Personality or Situation: Can Entrepreneurs be Created?* Paper presented at the meeting of the Eastern Psychological Association, New York, April (1991).

Sherman, Aliza Pilar. "Let's Have Some Funds!" *Entrepreneur* 32 No. 7 July (2004): 40.

Siropolis, N. C. *Small Business Management: A Guide to Entrepreneurship.* 4th edition. Boston: Houghton Mifflin, 1990.

Smigla, J. E. and G. Pastoria. "Emotional Intelligence: Some Have It, Others Can Learn." *The CPA Journal,* June 2000 v.6 i6 p60.

Smith, Rebecca. It Takes Courage. *Entrepreneur's Start-Ups Magazine.* June (2002): 1-4

Sobel, Robert. *The Great Boom, 1950-2000: How a Generation of Americans Created the World's Most Prosperous Society.* New York: St. Martin Press, 2000.

Spaeder, K. E. "What To Do When Your Entrepreneurial Brain is Working Overtime." *Entrepreneur Magazine*, December 2002.

Stafford, Diane. "It's Tough Being Your Own Boss." *The Kansas City Star*, July 4, 2004, final edition. KansasCity.com, http://www.kansascity.com/mld/kansascity/business/9071815.htm

Steedy, G. "Emotional Intelligence is key to Leadership." *Business First*. February 28, 2003.

Thompson, J. "Go for the Goal: A step-by-step guide to achieving your dreams." *Business Start-Ups Magazine*, April 1998.

Tiffany, Laura. "The Top 40 Homebased Business Resources" *HomeOfficeMag.com,* August 2000, http://www.Entrepreneur.com/article/0,4621,302180,00.html

Wahlgren, Eric. "The First Employee." *Inc. Magazine.* February (2004): 30-33.

Whalen, Matthew, Khin-Maung-Gyi, Felix, Smitlhwvick, David. "Leadership Style and Values Chart the Course for an Entrepreneurial Journey." *Journal of Organizational Excellence* 23 No. 2 Spring (2004): 43-50.

Wolter, Romanus. "Fear Factor: Does the idea of starting your own business paralyze you? We've got some simple techniques to get you back in control." *Entrepreneur Magazine.* June (2003): 1-5.

Women's Business Institute, Fargo, ND, April 1997.

Zahra, Shaker A., Hayton, James C., Salvato, Carlo. "Entrepreneurship Theory and Practice." *Entrepreneurship Theory and Practice* 28 no. 4 Summer (2004): 363-381.

About the Authors

Dulce M. Ramirez-Damon is a doctoral student at Florida International University and a former high school and elementary school teacher. She has over 13 years of retail sales and operations management experience. Dulce is Co-Founder of "Who's That Enterprises, Inc." She resides in Miami, Florida with her husband, Charles and son Charlie.

Concepcion L. Tuma is currently a doctoral student at Florida International University. Her educational background is in Business, MIS and Human Resources. She is the Co-Founder of "Who's That Enterprises, Inc." Concepcion currently resides in Miami, Florida with her family.

Index

0-595-33041-X